Praise for *Fearless Résumés*

"Marky cuts to the core of what it takes to quickly attract the eye of an interviewer. She skillfully guides readers through an ingenious step-by-step process leading to a powerful and uniquely customized résumé. Marky Stein's book is sure to be a winner for the serious job seeker."

—Lynn Joseph, Ph.D., bestselling author of
The Job-Loss Recovery Program Guide:
The Ultimate Visualization System for
Landing a Great Job Now,
www.DrLynnJoseph.com

"Marky Stein's latest book, *Fearless Résumés*, is aptly titled. She shows readers how to develop their 'power proposition' and then weave that into a clear and winning résumé. Her down-to-earth approach, along with numerous tips and examples, turns the process of résumé writing into a confidence building experience, leading to the creation of the ultimate, 'fearless' résumé. Readers will find this book to be of real value in innumerable practical and motivational ways."

—Mark Guterman, principal,
MeaningfulCareers.com and author,
Common Sense for Uncommon Times

"Marky Stein's book is ALL about sales. How to hit the employers' 'hot buttons' and get their attention right off the bat, how to keep them 'hooked' all through the résumé and how to dramatically increase the probability of 'closing' with an invitation to an interview. She's definitely got the strategy job seekers need today to win the important meetings and coveted job offers they desire."

—Mitchell Goozé, CSP,
Customer Manufacturing Group, Inc.,
author of *Value Acceleration: Secrets To Building*
An Unbeatable Competitive Advantage

Fearless
RÉSUMÉS

Fearless
RÉSUMÉS

The Proven Method for Getting a Great Job Fast

MARKY STEIN

New York   Chicago   San Francisco   Lisbon
London   Madrid   Mexico City   Milan   New Delhi
San Juan   Seoul   Singapore   Sydney   Toronto

ISBN: 978-0-07-148235-6
MHID: 0-07-148235-0

McGraw-Hill books are available at special quantity discounts to use as premiums and sales promotions, or for use in corporate training programs. To contact a representative, please e-mail us at bulksales@mcgraw-hill.com.

This book is printed on acid-free paper.

*This book is dedicated to
the magnificence in all of us.*

CONTENTS

ACKNOWLEDGMENTS

I wish to thank Rusty Stein, Jill Stein, Phil, Karyn, Susan and Diane Isaacs, Marty Bonsall, Gabrielle Antolovich, Patria Jacobs, Mary Glenn, Ed Chupak, Stu Levin, Daina Penikas, Monster.com, Dan Janal, McGraw-Hill, Aileen Haynes, Bali Stein, Tony Frank, Amy Frost, Lynn Joseph, Kate Smith, Grace Engel, Gerd Salmonson, Kevin Donlin and especially Melissa Greer. Your love and encouragement sustain me.

CHAPTER 1

Why Fearless Résumés?

"One must have the adventurous daring to accept oneself as a bundle of possibilities and undertake the most interesting game in the world—making the most of one's best."

—Harry Emerson Fosdick

Writing a résumé can really be scary! After all, unless all you have to do is fill out an application to get an interview, writing a résumé is just about the *only* way you have to get your foot in the door.

- Up until now, many doors may have been closed to you. You may not even have had the chance to go to an interview yet. You may be getting some interviews, but not the ones you really want. You may love your résumé or hate your résumé or not even have one, but those doors seem to be shut tighter and tighter. *Not for long.*

The guide you're holding is *not* a book about proper grammar or about making your résumé look "fancy" and expensive. Yes, those things may be nice, but we're going to take it just one step further.

A Strategic Approach to Writing Résumés

Fearless Résumés presents you with a *tested and unbeatable strategy*, proven time after time, to get people just like you the job offers you're dreaming of and working so hard to get.

Having personally tested the *Fearless Résumés* strategy on more than 15,000 clients since 1989, I'm here to take their successes and pass these job-seeking secrets on to you. You'll find this strategy for writing a résumé as simple, powerful, and effective as it was for those job seekers.

- I didn't say it would be easy, but I will tell you that writing your résumé will be far simpler than you ever imagined it could be.

Why?

Because I've boiled down what makes a résumé work to a few straightforward but extremely potent ideas that anyone, whether a student, at entry level, or an executive, can use.

In the few hours you spend reading this book and doing the concrete and practical exercises it contains, you're going to create a résumé that pries open those closely guarded doors and knocks them right down, allowing you to see and talk to the people you need to know in order to get the job or career that you've been striving so vigorously for.

A Brand New Approach to Résumé Writing

If you're at the bookstore, leafing through the many books on résumés that are for sale, you'll quickly see that *Fearless Résumés* is different from the others.

This is not just an ordinary résumé book, with hundreds of résumés for you to choose from and "customize" for yourself. In fact, this book takes an *utterly brand new and tested approach* to the often terrible task of crafting that all-important treatment.

As I said before, *Fearless Résumés* is going to teach you a carefully planned strategy, based upon what employers are *really* looking for, that will carry you through your job search, your interview, and finally to the offers you've been waiting for.

- It doesn't matter if writing a résumé or talking about yourself in an interview has been difficult or frustrating before.

You're going to learn a new and totally natural way to penetrate the employer's emotions, persuade his intelligence, and present yourself at your best. In the chapters that follow, you'll discover the secret of how employers, in fact, treat and look at your document.

You'll know the commonsense truth about what *really* motivates them, and it will make all the difference in what you say to them and how you say it in your Fearless Résumé.

In fact, it's been *proven* time and time again that using the secret you're about to learn will make employers pick up and pointedly concentrate on reading *your* Fearless Résumé at a moment's glance, while your competitors' résumés are swirling in the paper shredder.

I know you may have struggled with ordinary résumé writing before, and I know just how demoralizing and frustrating that can be. I know, too, that you may have spent hours and even days editing the résumé that you already have, but that just isn't delivering what you need or expect. You may feel puzzled about what to do and worried about whether you'll ever get the interviews or the job offers you want.

- You're not alone anymore in the task of creating this very important document that will influence the future of your work and your life. *Together*, you and I are going to wage an all-out war as an unstoppable team, and *we're going to win!*

How Can This Book Help You?

If you already have a résumé and you're getting lots of interviews with it, you may not need to read this book. Save your money and buy a few Starbucks coffees with it or take your best friend to lunch.

On the other hand, if your résumé *is* producing interviews for you, but you're having trouble in your interviews supporting what your résumé says about you, your résumé is probably not a good fit for you in the real world.

If that's the case, put a hold on that mocha chocolate nonfat extra foamy latte and invest in this book. You'll be very glad that you did.

- So, you may be worried that you really don't have a good existing résumé at all. You may also have a fear of writing your very *first* résumé or of crafting the document after being out of the job market for a while or changing your focus to a whole new industry.

You're going to learn how to tackle those problems and many more, but there may be a score of other worries you have about your résumé. Most people do. Let's look at some of them that will be answered for you as you progress through the pages of your new guide.

EXERCISE 1

Please check the box at the beginning of each paragraph on the list to figure out exactly how you feel about your own résumé needs.

Feel free to check more than one or to write your own version of your concerns at the end of this list.

☐ I have a résumé that was written by a professional or someone else, but that just doesn't seem to fit me. It looks well written, but I'm uncomfortable when I send it out and/or have to explain it at an interview.

☐ I have a résumé, and I've submitted it to many employers, including online, newspapers, and e-mail "blasts," but I'm *still* not getting any interviews. I feel frustrated!

☐ I have a great work history at good companies for over 25 years, and it's all documented on my résumé. Why isn't anyone calling me? Could I be the victim of age discrimination?

☐ I just graduated from school, and I don't have *any* "real" work experiences. Do odd jobs and internships count as work? I don't see how I can get hired if I've never been hired before. I don't have anything to write on a résumé. Can you help me?

☐ Several friends of mine, a recruiter, and a career counselor all told me that my résumé should be one page and *only* one page. I feel that I can't possibly condense all of my experience and other information onto one page without leaving out important accomplishments that I'm proud of. What should I do?

☐ I've had some bad luck with my employment history. It seems like I just start a job, and then in two or three months there's a layoff. I'm afraid that employers will think that I can't make a commitment, even though I would love to stay at a full-time permanent job for years if I had the chance. How can I solve this problem?

☐ I took some time out of my career to spend with my young family. I gave birth/helped my partner give birth to our infant son/daughter. I think that employers may be rejecting my résumé because of this gap in employment. My family is my top priority, but now it seems like I can't get back into the job market. I feel angry! I feel powerless about what to do.

☐ Last year I did some overseas travel and practiced my passion for photography at a community college. I didn't work for a year, and now it's harder than ever to get interviews. What can I do?

☐ I have reasons, such as health problems, an extended wedding and honeymoon, family illnesses, a painful divorce, or a disability, for gaps in employment. I don't want to lie, but is there any way to cover up these gaps?

☐ I feel that my résumé just looks dull. I haven't done anything that special in my life. I have nothing to brag about. I just did my job. But I can't get interviews. Is it because my résumé isn't good enough?

☐ I have all the experience in the world. I just don't have the degree that's needed for the jobs I'm applying for. I could run circles around half of those people with degrees, but I don't have a piece of paper to prove it. Am I really going to have to spend thousands of dollars and years of my life just to get a degree? Why can't I get hired when I have double the experience of these people with degrees?

☐ Every time I've gotten a job, either it's been through a friend or I just filled out a short application. Now I'm searching for a new job, and all those available require that I send a résumé. Help! I have no idea how to write a résumé.

☐ I got fired from a job—maybe even more than once. Can I just leave those jobs off my résumé in case they call the employers and find out that I was terminated? I'm really scared of a possible employer knowing about that/those incident(s).

☐ An employer or recruiter told me that I had a horrible résumé. Another one said it was great. It makes no sense to me. I'm confused. Which should I believe?

☐ I think I have a great résumé, but I've been looking for a job for over six months, and I know I have all the right qualifications. I just don't get interviews. I don't understand what I'm doing wrong. Any advice?

☐ This is my first time writing a résumé (*or*) I'm writing a brand new résumé for a new industry, location, or job change. I don't even know where to start.

☐ I've been on several interviews. They keep saying the same thing: I'm "overqualified." You'd think that was a *good* thing! What's wrong?

☐ Are there any other reasons that you find résumé writing scary? Write any other concerns you may have in the following spaces. *Let's solve them together!*

☐ _____
_____
_____
_____
_____
_____.

☐ _____
_____
_____
_____
_____
_____.

Did you find your own story in any of these questions? Well, if so, welcome! You're in the right place. If not, maybe you're reading this book for some other reason, and I'm glad you're here. We're about to go on a great adventure together.

This book, as I said, is not just a compilation of many different kinds of résumés. It is written with *you*, your concerns, and your career and livelihood in mind. It's not a book about the perfect model résumé. There is no such thing, and even career counselors still disagree about the best length, content, and format for a résumé. In fact, anyone who tells you that she'll write the perfect résumé for you or teach you how to write the perfect résumé is kidding herself.

- I can't promise you a flawless résumé. What I *can* promise is that you will start getting interviews.

What Can You Expect from This Book?

In the second chapter, "What Do Employers Really Want?" you're going to learn secrets about what *really* motivates employers when they pick up your résumé. By "tuning in" to both their conscious and their unconscious desires, you'll find out why it's important for you to "hook" your reader *instantly* and get him to take a look at the rest of your résumé.

In Chapter 3, you'll learn how to glue your employer to the page in less than seven seconds by using multiple hooks (words that emotionally attract employers).

I'll give plenty of examples of power propositions that have worked for real people, from those at entry level to managers to executives, in a wide range of positions and industries. Then, in Chapter 4, I'll walk you through the simple steps of drafting your own power proposition, something that is *guaranteed* to make you feel proud and unstoppable.

Your power proposition is going to be near the very top of your résumé (so that it will be the first thing seen by the reader). What about the rest of your résumé? It's important, too. Once you have the reader "hooked," you want to continue to rivet her attention on the rest of your skills, accomplishments, education, and work history.

The material in Chapters 5 and 6—identifying your skills, building a skills arsenal, and crafting what I call Q statements—will form the building blocks that make your résumé totally on target, irresistible to your reader, and absolutely unique.

Chapter 7 will show you how to organize these essential elements of your presentation into "blocks" of information; the contact block, the objective block, the summary block, the employment history block, the education and training block, and some optional blocks that will make it easy for the employer to see specific skills, awards, or achievements that make you right for the job.

In Chapter 8, I'll deliver the final ten tips that will eliminate most of the errors that people tend to make on résumés.

- Finally, in Chapter 9, using the building blocks you've mastered in the first eight chapters, it will be *your* time to turn out your first Fearless Résumé! Some sample résumés are given in Chapter 10.

For now, I have faith in you and the absolute conviction that you will triumph in your job search. You've got me on your side, so let's start right now.

CHAPTER 2

What Do Employers Really Want?

> "The truth of a thing is the feel of it, not the think of it."
> —Stanley Kubrick

Do you know that it takes only three to seven seconds for a reader to determine whether your résumé goes in the "yes" pile or gets deleted or thrown in a paper shredder? Well, it's true.

Over 17 years as a career coach in almost constant contact with employers, recruiters, human resources representatives, and, of course, job seekers gives me an inside view of what *really* goes on when you submit your résumé to a company or small business.

What's Going On Behind the Scenes?

It has been estimated that when a job is advertised in a major metropolitan newspaper and on a few key Internet job sites, a human resources staffer or hiring manager may have as many as 350 résumés crowding his inbox or the corner of his desk *on a daily basis*. Do you think that such a person reads every one of those résumés from start to finish? The answer, you may be surprised to find out, is no.

It takes a very special résumé to grab your reader's attention and keep her reading all the way through when she may have already seen and thrown away 200 résumés before getting to yours. *That's just the kind of résumé you're going to have by the end of this book.*

How, then, do we know how to write that special résumé? Did we learn it in school? Probably not. Did our parents show us how to do it? Maybe, but has the result worked for you? Have you ever read a book or seen a career counselor who could really tell you that magic formula that you could repeat, again and again, to achieve the same favorable results? If not, why not?

The fact is that too many people and the majority of books about résumés focus on the *résumé itself* rather than turning their target to deep down inside the *emotions* and the *mind* of the reader.

If you're going to get an interview by sending someone your résumé when they are almost 349 competitors a day up against you, you're going to need to know more than just how to write something neat and clean that lists your job history on it; you need inside, tested, and proven particulars about how to make that employer pick your résumé.

- The inside of the hiring proccss and the interior of employers' emotions are exactly those untapped, "secret" solutions to the problems of getting the interviews that I'm going to share with you right now.

To grab your reader in the first few seconds, to get her to read the whole page or two and then get her to take *action*, we're going to use the power of what I've named *résumé psychology*.

What Is Résumé Psychology?

Résumé psychology is the study and practice of using words in a prescribed document (your résumé) to get a reader to

1. Feel something
2. Think something
3. Do something

To express this chain of events as succinctly as possible, you can imagine the events taking place in this order and in a manner such as this:

Phase 1 (three to seven seconds): The reader will first *feel*, consciously or unconsciously, that you are going to help him.

Phase 2 (one to five minutes): He will then *think* that you are going to make money (or its equivalent) for his company.

Phase 3: Finally, he will be compelled to *do* something about it—that is, to discuss your résumé with his boss or just pick up the phone himself and call you.

Phase 1 *must* work if you are to get to Phase 2. Phase 3 *cannot* happen unless Phase 2 is complete. Therefore, your first task is to win the employer's emotions and get her to feel that you are on *her* side—that you are going to help her in some way.

Logic or Emotions?

One would hope that résumé readers would base their decisions on logic or rationality, carefully weighing the qualifications written on your résumé against the requirements of the position that you're applying for. We may imagine that this is true, but that is not how the human brain works. *An initial reaction is always emotional.*

- Once I show you how to influence the person's feelings (emotions), thinking (cognitions), and actions (behavior), you can bet that your phone will start ringing as expectant employers want to meet you.

Winning the Reader's Favor

To accomplish this, we're going take a peek inside the employer's brain before you even set pen to paper to craft your document. By mastering what the employer actually *sees* in the first seven seconds of laying eyes on your page and how it affects the *emotional* part of his brain, you're going to learn how to keep him reading down the page while other people's résumés are whirling in the paper shredder.

- Together, in this chapter, we're going to answer the question you may already be asking yourself: "What do employers *really* want, anyway?"

In *Fearless Résumés*, you're going to quickly learn what we now know about how human beings read and process information. We're going to use these powerful pieces of what psychology tells us about human perception to your advantage.

We're going to harness *résumé psychology* to put you on the fast track to winning an interview and getting a new job, and it all begins in a fraction of a second. Am I saying that someone's mind can make a snap decision about my résumé immediately? Yes!

Résumé psychology says that your résumé will be judged 80 percent on what the reader sees in the first few lines and about 20 percent on what appears in the rest of the résumé.

In fact, every single reader knows within just a few seconds whether you are likely to help her *meet her needs* or are likely to threaten her efforts.

14

The "Seven-Second" Zone

Psychologists say that we "know" in a split second (about 1/16 second, to be exact) whether *anything* that comes into our environment is going to help or threaten our instinct to survive.

This split-second test of whether something is good for us or bad for us is a top task of our brains and nervous systems because it governs our very survival. Say that it takes only 1/16 second (what psychologists call a "slice") for us to tell this. Whether it's an object, a car, a person, climate change, or even a piece of paper like your résumé, it will be evaluated by your brain at lightning speed.

Compared to 1/16 second, seven full seconds seems like an eon! Yet, that's all you have to snare the survival instinct of your reader and get her to salivate over the contents of your offering. If you miss that chance, you may never be able to recover it.

During this critical "seven-second zone," the brain is bombarded with impulses whose only purpose is to determine one thing: *is this (object, person, situation) going to pose danger to me or help me?*

You know yourself that a feeling of friendship, affection, intense dislike, or even "falling in love" can happen the moment you lay eyes on someone or something.

We're going to capitalize on those powerful feelings in the next chapter with something that I call a *power proposition*. Your power proposition, which the reader will see in that crucial seven-second zone, will rivet her to your résumé.

- With only the words in one powerful paragraph (about four to seven sentences), you will infuse the reader's nerve cells with energy and curiosity. In brief, you make the employer "fall in love" with you!

So just how are you going to strike up a "romance" with the employer that has the potential of blossoming into a long-term love affair (your new job)? Well, as with most romances and even great friendships, it's essential, as we've said, to make a good first impression.

On paper, you don't have your smile, your face, or the sparkle in your eye to let someone know that you're friendly and attractive. You don't even have the friendly, provocative, or interesting tone of voice to offer that you might have if you met someone face-to-face or on the telephone.

On your résumé, all you've got that can evoke positive feelings in the reader is the written word, and it's those words—especially the first few sentences that the reader encounters—that are going to make all the difference.

Your Power Proposition

What you'll soon come to know as a power proposition is a forceful, confident, and concise paragraph that contains one or more "hooks" that your reader will find irresistible.

- These hooks, if you will, are words that express how well you can fulfill the employer's *financial, business, personal,* and *emotional* needs.

Think we can do all that in just a few lines? The answer is yes, and in the next chapter you'll see just how easy it really is.

Once you are clear about the statements you'll make in your power proposition, you'll also be clear about *how you can uniquely solve the problems faced by the employer and thereby satisfy one or more of her desires.*

Here is a list of the things that almost every employer either wants to have or wants to avoid. All of these things, at the bottom line, affect his ingrained sense of survival.

WHAT MOTIVATES YOUR READER?

- Greater profits
- Less waste of time, labor, money, and materials
- A cleaner, better organized, and safer workplace
- Better employee morale and commitment
- Improved recruiting, hiring, and employee retention
- Sturdier and more innovative technologies, machines, and instruments

- Recording and storing detailed and accurate information
- Keeping customers and clients happy
- Greater marketability and sales appeal for her products
- Better public perception of her company and its services and goods

The Key to Knowing about Survival Needs

When you, by your efforts at work, *increase* anything that the employer sees as valuable and *decrease* things that the employer sees as dangerous, you are fulfilling his primal needs for *safety, security,* and *well-being.*

- You show him that you can do this by writing a résumé that presents a variety of "tasty" hooks. Your power proposition contains the initial hooks.

A power proposition is easy to write, yet deceptively attractive. Once you know what's required to spark an attraction in the employer's brain, you'll have a lifelong tool that will help you not only with your résumé, but also with your interview and other parts of your job search.

How about moving on to constructing a paragraph that will rivet your reader's eyes to the page and, most important, fill her with a pleasant sense of anticipation?

CHAPTER 3

Rivet the Reader in the First Seven Seconds

"When love and skill work together, expect a masterpiece."

—John Ruskin

This chapter may be among the most important pieces of advice on résumés that you've ever seen. Read on and you'll find out why.

Multiple Uses of a Power Proposition

When you master making your power proposition come alive, you'll know how to capture the attention of your reader instantly. And there's more!

You're *also* going to be prepared for the interview question, "Tell me about yourself," as well as for other questions regarding your skills, strengths, and accomplishments. Not only will this special paragraph guide your résumé and aid you in interviewing, but you're going to be able to use *parts* of your power proposition to describe yourself to perfect strangers who may have job leads for you and to people you meet socially or in your job-hunting network.

- Your power proposition, because it is a rich mini-snapshot of yourself and what you can do, may indeed become one of the most critical tools in your job-seeking technique.

Let's get focused and learn how to harness the energy in the first few sentences of your résumé to get the employer on the hook. Are you ready?

Steps to Writing Your Power Proposition

In this chapter, we're going to prepare you to create your own personal power proposition.

First, I want you to look at several different power propositions so that you can observe how they fall into particular, predictable patterns, even though each is describing a very different position. In the next chapter, we'll write the paragraph in a predictable step-by-step process.

This process is moving toward a very worthy goal: a paragraph that will irresistibly influence your reader to take action. Here are 12 sample power propositions. Don't worry if the wording or the structure seems unfamiliar at first. This is "résumé talk."

We don't use the word *I* or *me*, and sometimes we simply use phrases rather than what one would consider "proper" English grammar.

All in all, it's not the punctuation that counts—it's the words that represent what we know from résumé psychology to be the very words the employer is looking for.

Once you read all of these power propositions and the additional ones from the sample résumés in Chapter 7, you're going to have a good feeling about expressing yourself in this way, and the style will be far more familiar to you.

Sample Power Propositions

Power Proposition 1

CUSTOMER SERVICE MANAGER

Over three years' experience as a customer service representative and manager serving small to medium-sized companies, specializing in retail sales, inventory control, and employee training. Designed and delivered trainings for up to 20 participants while working at Home Design Warehouse. Awarded for perfect cash drawers over 12 times in a five-year period. Voted Customer Service Manager of the Month in July 2006 and February 2008. A.A. in Business Administration from Silva Valley College. Certificate in Retail Management from University of New York extension program. Organized, friendly, and detail-oriented.

Now, has this candidate provided the bait for the hooks that will catch the reader's attention and lock it there until he has finished reading the whole résumé?

Of course she has. This little paragraph, her power proposition, answers not only the *minimum requirements* (and preferences) of the position that are spelled out in the job description, but indicates even more fertile talent than is expected.

Power Proposition 2

DIRECTOR OF STRATEGIC MARKETING

Over 10 years' director-level experience in strategic marketing, specializing in strategic planning, team leadership, and driving business development in the high-tech Fortune 100 sector. Executed multimillion-dollar deals of up to $4.5 million with global partners by developing long-term customer/partner relationships, directing multifunctional teams of up to 90 for projects with budgets of up to $75 million, and creating and developing company strategic framework and plans for expanding into new target markets. MSEE, Yale University; MBA with concentration in Marketing/Finance, Cornell University. Member of International Association of Marketing Professionals. Awarded the Trendsetter Award in 2007 for Innovation in Strategic Marketing from the American Marketing Association

Power Proposition 3

COMPUTER NETWORK ADMINISTRATOR

Proficient computer network administrator in the manufacturing industry, specializing in UNIX and Linox platforms, troubleshooting and configuration of local area networks. Supervised the team of 16 technicians for a larger Fortune 500 company that reduced downtime for the manufacturer by 33 percent in the first year, thereby preventing almost 140 lost hours per week. Certified computer network IT administrator from Howard Vocational Technology School. Associate degree in Electronics from Hillsdale College.

Power Proposition 4

SALES AND MARKETING MANAGER

Over eight years as senior sales and marketing manager in health care and biomedical devices fields, specializing in prospecting, presentations, and talent acquisition. In five years while at Dullard Insurance Inc., developed marketing collateral that was partially responsible for the 67% surge in state sales during the years 2003 to 2008. Received several diamond awards for sales and marketing while at Dullard, including recognition as Diamond Professional in the years 2005 and 2008. B.A. in journalism; M.B.A. from Chicago State University with an emphasis in international marketing.

Power Proposition 5

PRODUCTION SUPERVISOR

Over 5 years' experience as a production supervisor/assistant manager in the manufacturing and retail industries, specializing in team leadership, operations, quality control, and employee training. Selected career accomplishments: exceeded production objective by a 25% increase in efficiency and 50% reduction in injuries. B.S. in Industrial Technology; training in TQM.

Power Propostion 6

FILM PRODUCTION MANAGER

Over 6 years as a production manager and assistant director on more than 11 feature films, specializing in hiring, logistics, and budgeting films of up to $24 million.

Saved 22% of the planned budget on *Dinner with a Thief* (Sammy T. Productions) by instituting second unit shooting at a second location. Cut 7 days of shooting by tightening deadlines using Quick Story software, resulting in a total saving of $210,000 from an $18 million budget. Bachelor's degree in Media and Communications, Florida State University at Orlando.

What if I Have Little or No Experience on the Job?

Even if you have less than a year of experience or no experience at all, there are ways we can express your knowledge in a way that still hooks the employers:

Knowledge of the field of _____ gained from *volunteer/internship/study* of _____, specializing in _____, _____, and _____.

So, if you're a recent college graduate, you may say something like that in the following power propositions.

Power Proposition 7

ENTRY-LEVEL COMPUTER ENGINEER

Knowledge of the field of computer engineering gained from 4 years of study and a B.S. in Computer Sciences, with classes in software engineering, Web design, and hardware troubleshooting. Got an A in Web design. Created a 90-page Web site using Flash design elements. Served as the president of the campus Computer Club. Dependable, detail-oriented, willing to learn.

Here's another for someone with a background as a volunteer.

Power Proposition 8

PRESCHOOL TEACHER

Six months' experience as a preschool aide gained from volunteer experience, specializing in play supervision, preparing meals, and reading to children. Handled groups of up to 15 children under the direction of the preschool director. Currently enrolled in a course of study leading to an A.A. degree in Early Childhood Education. Warm, fun, outgoing.

How about if you've had unpaid (or minimally paid) experience on the job for less than one year as an intern?

Power Proposition 9

ENTRY-LEVEL PHYSICAL THERAPIST ASSISTANT

Competence as a physical therapist assistant gained from earning a certificate in physical therapist assistant program at Hunter Community College, specializing in following treatment plans, kinesiology, and patient psychology. Completed an externship with excellent references at Simeone Sports Medicine and Chronic Pain Clinic in Lexington, Vermont. Carried a patient load of 10 under the supervision of the physical therapy director. Trustworthy, knowledgeable, great patient rapport. Graduated in the top 10 percent of the class at Hunter Community College.

What if you built your own home from scratch and made it energy-efficient or "green," but did not get paid for it?

What if you rigged your home with solar surfaces and wind turbines so well that you did not need conventional electricity at all? All that skill, effort, and knowledge does not have to be reserved for your personal life. If you wanted a job in sustainable energy, solar energy, or (the latest term) "green" technology, you could certainly say that you were *proficient* in the areas of construction, plumbing, tiling, building solar panels, installing special insulation, and a host of other skills that you gained while building a home for yourself. You could then use your proficiency in your power proposition.

Power Propostion 10

SUSTAINABLE ENERGY CONSULTANT

Proficiency in building green technology homes gained from building a 13,000-square-foot home in California that is independent of the traditional energy grid. Saved approximately $2,100 per month on electricity costs alone and an additional $300 for saved water usage.

Landscaped the home with 12 varieties of low-maintenance native plants and planted and maintained a vegetable and herb garden that is 20 square feet. Certificate in Sustainable Energy Planning from University of California Extension Program.

Power Proposition 11

ENTRY-LEVEL VIDEO CAMERA OPERATOR (STUDENT)

Competent video camera operator specializing in multicamera shoots, lighting, and editing. As an intern, worked on 1 hour and 55 minute documentary film about global warming and was hired again by the same company for a stipend to do lighting for a studio shoot on gifted children. Student film, *Capture of the Giants*, was voted "most popular student film" in 2006 at Xavier University. A.A. in theater arts, B.A. in film and television arts, Xavier University.

Power Proposition 12

ENTRY-LEVEL OFFICE MANAGER

Knowledge of office management in the medical field, specializing in customer care database creation, filing, billing, and coding gained from successful completion of a Certificate in Medical Office Management. Expert in Microsoft Office suite, including Microsoft Office Access. Earned an A-plus in medical terminology courses at Keller Community College, Orlando, Florida. Advanced Certificate in Office Management from Keller Community College.

Some other useful phrases to start off the first sentence of your power proposition are

Externship in (medical assisting)

Internship as a(n) (associate editor)

Apprenticeship as a(n) (electrician)

Okay, you've just seen several power propositions. Are you impressed?

Did you ever get a strange feeling that some of the people who wrote these were bragging?

That's not an uncommon response for someone who's writing a résumé. Bragging is exaggeration mixed with deceit. All of the power propositions you just read are simply facts. How can you brag when you're just telling the truth?

Is a shopkeeper bragging when he displays his finest merchandise in the store window?

Of course not. He, like you, is putting his most attractive wares out front for you to see in hopes that you'll come into the store, look more closely, and then buy something. It's the same with your power proposition. You're putting your best foot forward right away to attract the employer with the hope that she will read your résumé and call you for an interview.

Now that you've accepted that you're going to *have* to say some really good things about yourself, let's get to the next chapter and I'll walk you through writing each part of your own power proposition, step by step.

CHAPTER 4

Your Power Proposition

> "The best bet is to bet on yourself."
>
> —Arnold Glasgow

I'm sure that in reading the paragraphs in the last chapter, you noticed that all of them are constructed in the same or a very similar way. There is structure to a power proposition—a beginning, a middle, and an end.

- That's what makes a power proposition so easy to write. Every sentence and every part has a specific purpose.

Parts of a Power Proposition

This section gives a power proposition that's divided into nine parts, with some of the information left blank. Before each blank space, there is a number in parentheses.

We're going to talk about what kind of data goes after each number. Before you know it, you're going to have a power proposition of your own!

Writing your power proposition is just as easy as filling in the three to nine blank spaces.

- A power proposition has three *mandatory* ("must have") statements and four *optional* sentences.

I'll explain exactly how each part works so that you'll know how to fill in the blanks with tempting hooks that *grab* the reader in the first seven seconds.

Model Power Proposition

You don't need to write anything in the blank spaces now. After you take a peek at this model, I'll explain to you how to do it for yourself.

First Sentence

Write your level/years of experience, job title, industry(ies), and special skills.

Over (1) _____ years as a(n) (2) _____ in the
(3) _____ [optional] industry(ies), specializing in

(4) _____, _____,
and _____.

Second Sentence

Write an accomplishment here: (5)

_____
_____
_____.

You may choose to write another accomplishment here,
but this is optional:

_____
_____
_____.

Third and Further Sentences

Use one to four of the following:

Your degree(s) and/or certifications. (6)

_____
_____.

Your awards and/or special recognitions. (7)

_____
_____.

Memberships in professional organizations. (8)

_____
_____.

Personal characteristics. (9)

_____
_____.

What Does Each Part Mean?

Each sentence in your power proposition communicates something very important to the employer and has a potential hook (or many hooks) to grab his attention within the first seven seconds. Let's take each sentence and section one by one, and soon you'll have a completed paragraph.

Sentence 1, Blank 1: Level or Years of Experience

The first sentence indicates the number of years or level of experience you have doing a certain type of job.

- Remember from the previous chapter that if you have less than one year of experience, unpaid experience, or no paid working experience at all, you can start off with words like *competent, knowledgeable, proficient, volunteer, intern(ship), residency, externship, apprenticeship,* or *classroom study.*

For those with paid experience in the workplace, the first sentence would begin with the number of years of experience you've accumulated in your field. Listing anywhere from one to ten years is fine. Ten years of experience is enough to show that you are at the highest level of your job.

Listing more than 10 to 15 years of experience, however temping it is to show your professionalism, may consciously or unconsciously cause the reader to reject your résumé because of an unfortunate epidemic in some societies called *ageism.*

AGEISM

What is ageism? People are *wrongly* convinced that a more mature person may not stay long, may be unhealthy on the job, might get bored, could have trouble being supervised by a younger manager, or may demand higher pay.

Even though studies have proved these beliefs to be dead wrong, many employers persist in harboring these inexcusable and damaging myths. Until we as a society do the work of ridding ourselves of this very wrong form of discrimination based on age, it is wise not to risk an employer's concluding that he does not want to interview you because of his conscious or unconscious belief in ageism. The *only* reason to list something more than 10 years ago is if it is absolutely necessary to support your job target.

So let's keep your years of experience down to 10, or 15 at the most.

In Chapter 10, "Sample Résumés," I'll show you how to represent important positions that you may have held 16 or more years ago.

Sentence 1, Blank 2: My Job Title or Titles

Enter the job titles you've had over the span of your experience. For example, you could say any one of these things and still be expressing your expertise to the employer:

- Director of operations
- Upper management position in operations
- Executive position in operations
- X years' experience as an operations professional

SENTENCE 1, BLANK 3: THE INDUSTRY OR INDUSTRIES I'VE WORKED IN

The blank after the number (3) in the model represents the industry or industries you've worked in. You may look at the end of this chapter for a list of industries you might like to use in this spot.

- Listing an industry is optional and can simply be used to *clarify* or *strengthen* a job title. This is optional, but it is commonly used if you're staying in the same industry but going for a different job title in that industry.

EXERCISE 2

Please write the information for the first three blanks in the first sentence of your power proposition here:

1. _____

2. _____

3. _____

Wow, congratulations! In less than the blink of an eye, you've already told an employer your level of experience, a job title, and an industry! Unlike with traditional résumés, the employer will not have to go to all the trouble of scrolling down through the dates of your job history to determine how many years you've been at it.

You *already* have at least one and potentially three hooks into her.

Sentence #1, Three Blanks Marked 4:
My Skills, Strengths, and Specialties

The second part of the first sentence deals with your specialties.

- What are some of the things you do well and some of the things you like doing that pertain to your job target?

Do you have a job description in front of you? If so, use it. It will probably contain five to ten skills or areas of knowledge that the employer is looking for.

If any of your skills exactly *match* the job description, pick out the three that you most enjoy doing or are best at and write them in the specialty section. This is great bait for a hungry employer.

If you'd like some more ideas for skill words, refer to the lists of skills in Chapter 5. You'll be pleasantly surprised to find that you have many more skills than you've ever imagined. Every one of these skills is a potential hook for the right employer.

- Now you have your first sentence, and just look at how much information you've transmitted to the employer in such a short reading/time span!

Sentence #2 (and 3—optional)

The next two sentences contain descriptions of past accomplishments that you are proud of and/or that relate to the job you're applying for. What is the difference between a skill and an accomplishment?

Well, a skill is a word or phrase indicating something that you *can* do, like management, assembly, diagnosis, or writing reports. Accomplishments are specific ways in which you *used* your skills in the real world.

WRITING AN ACCOMPLISHMENT

For example, in the following sentences, the skill is underlined and the rest of the sentence describes an accomplishment.

<u>Managed</u> the finance department for a large grocery chain.

<u>Assembled</u> semiconductors for use in a defense company.

<u>Diagnosed</u> and <u>treated</u> over six patients per day in a private clinic.

<u>Wrote reports</u> on the earthquake preparedness of government buildings.

So, for the next exercise, I'm going to ask you to *pencil* in at least one accomplishment. If you can think of two, that's great, but the second one is optional for this exercise.

We're going to use these accomplishments as placeholders for now, because in the nest chapter, you're going to learn a proven way to make your accomplishments *really* shine.

EXERCISE 3

Please write one or two accomplishments in the following spaces:

Accomplishment:

_____

_____

_____

_____.

Accomplishment:

_____

_____

_____

_____.

CHANGING AN ACCOMPLISHMENT TO A Q STATEMENT

We're going to use the accomplishments you just listed as a foundation to construct statements that are at the very heart of your work history.

They are called *Q statements*, and they usually include numbers, percentages, and/or *very specific* information that appeals to virtually *every* employer's survival instinct.

We'll come back after the next chapter and turn your penciled-in accomplishments into Q statements that will reflect not only what you did, but the results that you produced.

Right now, I hope you've created at least one accomplishment and penciled it in. Great! We're almost finished with your unique power proposition, something that is essential for your Fearless Résumé.

- You'll find that your proposition also has an unmistakable "ring" to it when you actually *say* it in an interview, or even to someone who may have a job lead for you in an informal setting.

At this point, don't worry if you're thinking to yourself, "I just did my job. I really don't have anything that special to say." Most people think that at first.

As you learn more, you'll feel firsthand that once you learn how to turn skills into accomplishments and accomplishments into Q statements, as thousands of people have, your résumé and your interviewing skills are going to hit the sky, and your confidence, both on paper and in person, is going to soar.

Now, there are a few more optional sentences in your power proposition. We'll discuss those next.

Further Sentences

In the last sentences, you can add short phrases or sentences relating to one or all of the following:

1. Your education, training, certificates, or licenses, or education that you are still enrolled in. For example,

   Masters in Business Administration with an emphasis in Finance

Currently enrolled in a course of study leading to a Bachelor's Degree in Information Sciences

2. Awards, excellent grade point averages, or recognitions. For example,

   Awarded Salesperson of the Year in 2007

   Graduated with a 3.85 grade point average from Millman City College

3. Professional or student associations, organizations, or clubs that pertain to the position for which you're applying. For example,

   Society for Human Resource Management

   Event Planning Association of America

Now, I can't wait for you to see your whole power proposition on paper. You can make it very simple for now and add other parts that you want later. Remember, you don't have to fill in all of the blanks.

EXERCISE 4
First Draft of My Own Power Proposition

Over _____ years as a(n) _____ in the

_____ industry, specializing in

_____,

_____, and

_____. [Accomplishment(s)]:

_____

_____

_____.

_____

_____. [Education, awards, personal traits, etc.]

37

Your Finished Power Proposition

You may have drafted this version of your proposition in a way that's very similar to the way it's written in the book, *or* you may have already chosen your own wording that you feel comfortable with. As a test, please read the sentence *as if you were an employer*.

How long did it take you to read it? Three seconds? Ten seconds? What's important for you to understand is that in well under 10 seconds, you have *already* told the employer a lot about you.

Traditional résumés may have taken two pages—about two minutes *past* our employer's initial attention span—to say what you've said in less than 10 seconds.

In fact, it is customary (though not always) for educational qualifications to be left until the very end of the résumé. We don't want to take the risk that the employer won't read all that way, so we're going to put your education into your power proposition if it seems relevant, and it almost always does.

- You've already won your employer over. Congratulations! She won't have seen anyone give her so much useful information—in fact, the *exact* information she's looking for—in so little time.

In the next chapters, we're going to identify some of the skills that form the foundation of Q statements. Then, we're going to put a "spin" on those penciled-in accomplishments that you just wrote: we're going to turn them into Q statements. Now let's use them to deal the final blow.

List of Industries

Taken from http://www.sec.gov/info/edgar/siccodes.htm.

100	9	AGRICULTURAL PRODUCTION—CROPS
200	5	AGRICULTURAL PROD—LIVESTOCK & ANIMAL SPECIALTIES
700	9	AGRICULTURAL SERVICES
800	5	FORESTRY
900	9	FISHING, HUNTING AND TRAPPING
1000	4	METAL MINING
1040	4	GOLD AND SILVER ORES
1090	4	MISCELLANEOUS METAL ORES
1220	4	BITUMINOUS COAL & LIGNITE MINING
1221	4	BITUMINOUS COAL & LIGNITE SURFACE MINING
1311	4	CRUDE PETROLEUM & NATURAL GAS
1381	4	DRILLING OIL & GAS WELLS
1382	4	OIL & GAS FIELD EXPLORATION SERVICES
1389	4	OIL & GAS FIELD SERVICES, NEC
1400	4	MINING & QUARRYING OF NONMETALLIC MINERALS (NO FUELS)
1520	6	GENERAL BLDG CONTRACTORS— RESIDENTIAL BLDGS
1531	6	OPERATIVE BUILDERS
1540	6	GENERAL BLDG CONTRACTORS— NONRESIDENTIAL BLDGS
1600	6	HEAVY CONSTRUCTION OTHER THAN BLDG CONST—CONTRACTORS
1623	6	WATER, SEWER, PIPELINE, COMM & POWER LINE CONSTRUCTION

1700	6	CONSTRUCTION—SPECIAL TRADE CONTRACTORS
1731	6	ELECTRICAL WORK
2000	4	FOOD AND KINDRED PRODUCTS
2011	5	MEAT PACKING PLANTS
2013	5	SAUSAGES & OTHER PREPARED MEAT PRODUCTS
2015	5	POULTRY SLAUGHTERING AND PROCESSING
2020	4	DAIRY PRODUCTS
2024	4	ICE CREAM & FROZEN DESSERTS
2030	4	CANNED, FROZEN & PRESERVD FRUIT, VEG & FOOD SPECIALTIES
2033	4	CANNED FRUITS, VEG, PRESERVES, JAMS & JELLIES
2040	4	GRAIN MILL PRODUCTS
2050	4	BAKERY PRODUCTS
2052	4	COOKIES & CRACKERS
2060	4	SUGAR & CONFECTIONERY PRODUCTS
2070	4	FATS & OILS
2080	9	BEVERAGES
2082	9	MALT BEVERAGES
2086	9	BOTTLED & CANNED SOFT DRINKS & CARBONATED WATERS
2090	4	MISCELLANEOUS FOOD PREPARATIONS & KINDRED PRODUCTS
2092	4	PREPARED FRESH OR FROZEN FISH & SEAFOODS
2100	5	TOBACCO PRODUCTS
2111	5	CIGARETTES

2200	2	TEXTILE MILL PRODUCTS
2211	2	BROADWOVEN FABRIC MILLS, COTTON
2221	2	BROADWOVEN FABRIC MILLS, MAN MADE FIBER & SILK
2250	2	KNITTING MILLS
2253	9	KNIT OUTERWEAR MILLS
2273	2	CARPETS & RUGS
2300	9	APPAREL & OTHER FINISHD PRODS OF FABRICS & SIMILAR MATL
2320	9	MEN'S & BOYS' FURNISHGS, WORK CLOTHG, & ALLIED GARMENTS
2330	9	WOMEN'S, MISSES', AND JUNIORS' OUTERWEAR
2340	9	WOMEN'S, MISSES', CHILDREN'S & INFANTS' UNDERGARMENTS
2390	9	MISCELLANEOUS FABRICATED TEXTILE PRODUCTS
2400	6	LUMBER & WOOD PRODUCTS (NO FURNITURE)
2421	6	SAWMILLS & PLANTING MILLS, GENERAL
2430	6	MILLWOOD, VENEER, PLYWOOD, & STRUCTURAL WOOD MEMBERS
2451	6	MOBILE HOMES
2452	6	PREFABRICATED WOOD BLDGS & COMPONENTS
2510	6	HOUSEHOLD FURNITURE
2511	6	WOOD HOUSEHOLD FURNITURE (NO UPHOLSTERED)
2520	6	OFFICE FURNITURE
2522	6	OFFICE FURNITURE (NO WOOD)

2531	6	PUBLIC BLDG & RELATED FURNITURE
2540	6	PARTITIONS, SHELVG, LOCKERS, & OFFICE & STORE FIXTURES
2590	6	MISCELLANEOUS FURNITURE & FIXTURES
2600	9	PAPERS & ALLIED PRODUCTS
2611	9	PULP MILLS
2621	9	PAPER MILLS
2631	9	PAPERBOARD MILLS
2650	9	PAPERBOARD CONTAINERS & BOXES
2670	9	CONVERTED PAPER & PAPERBOARD PRODS (NO CONTAINERS/BOXES)
2673	6	PLASTICS, FOIL & COATED PAPER BAGS
2711	5	NEWSPAPERS: PUBLISHING OR PUBLISHING & PRINTING
2721	5	PERIODICALS: PUBLISHING OR PUBLISHING & PRINTING
2731	5	BOOKS: PUBLISHING OR PUBLISHING & PRINTING
2732	5	BOOK PRINTING
2741	5	MISCELLANEOUS PUBLISHING
2750	5	COMMERCIAL PRINTING
2761	5	MANIFOLD BUSINESS FORMS
2771	5	GREETING CARDS
2780	5	BLANKBOOKS, LOOSELEAF BINDERS, & BOOKBINDG & RELATD WORK
2790	5	SERVICE INDUSTRIES FOR THE PRINTING TRADE
2800	6	CHEMICALS & ALLIED PRODUCTS
2810	6	INDUSTRIAL INORGANIC CHEMICALS

2820	6	PLASTIC MATERIAL, SYNTH RESIN/RUBBER, CELLULOS (NO GLASS)
2821	6	PLASTIC MATERIALS, SYNTH RESINS & NONVULCAN ELASTOMERS
2833	1	MEDICINAL CHEMICALS & BOTANICAL PRODUCTS
2834	1	PHARMACEUTICAL PREPARATIONS
2835	1	IN VITRO & IN VIVO DIAGNOSTIC SUBSTANCES
2836	1	BIOLOGICAL PRODUCTS (NO DIAGNOSTIC SUBSTANCES)
2840	6	SOAP, DETERGENTS, CLEANG PREPARATIONS, PERFUMES, COSMETICS
2842	6	SPECIALTY CLEANING, POLISHING AND SANITATION PREPARATIONS
2844	6	PERFUMES, COSMETICS, & OTHER TOILET PREPARATIONS
2851	6	PAINTS, VARNISHES, LACQUERS, ENAMELS & ALLIED PRODS
2860	6	INDUSTRIAL ORGANIC CHEMICALS
2870	5	AGRICULTURAL CHEMICALS
2890	6	MISCELLANEOUS CHEMICAL PRODUCTS
2891	6	ADHESIVES & SEALANTS
2911	4	PETROLEUM REFINING
2950	6	ASPHALT PAVING & ROOFING MATERIALS
2990	6	MISCELLANEOUS PRODUCTS OF PETROLEUM & COAL
3011	6	TIRES & INNER TUBES
3021	6	RUBBER & PLASTICS FOOTWEAR
3050	6	GASKETS, PACKG & SEALG DEVICES & RUBBER & PLASTICS HOSE

3060	6	FABRICATED RUBBER PRODUCTS, NEC
3080	6	MISCELLANEOUS PLASTICS PRODUCTS
3081	6	UNSUPPORTED PLASTICS FILM & SHEET
3086	6	PLASTICS FOAM PRODUCTS
3089	6	PLASTICS PRODUCTS, NEC
3100	9	LEATHER & LEATHER PRODUCTS
3140	9	FOOTWEAR (NO RUBBER)
3211	6	FLAT GLASS
3220	6	GLASS & GLASSWARE, PRESSED OR BLOWN
3221	6	GLASS CONTAINERS
3231	6	GLASS PRODUCTS, MADE OF PURCHASED GLASS
3241	6	CEMENT, HYDRAULIC
3250	6	STRUCTURAL CLAY PRODUCTS
3260	6	POTTERY & RELATED PRODUCTS
3270	6	CONCRETE, GYPSUM & PLASTER PRODUCTS
3272	6	CONCRETE PRODUCTS, EXCEPT BLOCK & BRICK
3281	6	CUT STONE & STONE PRODUCTS
3290	6	ABRASIVE, ASBESTOS & MISC NONMETALLIC MINERAL PRODS
3310	6	STEEL WORKS, BLAST FURNACES & ROLLING & FINISHING MILLS
3312	6	STEEL WORKS, BLAST FURNACES & ROLLING MILLS (COKE OVENS)
3317	6	STEEL PIPE & TUBES
3320	6	IRON & STEEL FOUNDRIES
3330	4	PRIMARY SMELTING & REFINING OF NONFERROUS METALS

3334	4	PRIMARY PRODUCTION OF ALUMINUM
3341	6	SECONDARY SMELTING & REFINING OF NONFERROUS METALS
3350	6	ROLLING, DRAWING, & EXTRUDING OF NONFERROUS METALS
3357	6	DRAWING & INSULATING OF NONFERROUS WIRE
3360	6	NONFERROUS FOUNDRIES (CASTINGS)
3390	6	MISCELLANEOUS PRIMARY METAL PRODUCTS
3411	6	METAL CANS
3412	6	METAL SHIPPING BARRELS, DRUMS, KEGS & PAILS
3420	6	CUTLERY, HANDTOOLS & GENERAL HARDWARE
3430	6	HEATING EQUIP, EXCEPT ELEC & WARM AIR; & PLUMBING FIXTURES
3433	6	HEATING EQUIPMENT, EXCEPT ELECTRIC & WARM AIR FURNACES
3440	6	FABRICATED STRUCTURAL METAL PRODUCTS
3442	6	METAL DOORS, SASH, FRAMES, MOLDINGS & TRIM
3443	6	FABRICATED PLATE WORK (BOILER SHOPS)
3444	6	SHEET METAL WORK
3448	6	PREFABRICATED METAL BUILDINGS & COMPONENTS
3451	6	SCREW MACHINE PRODUCTS
3452	6	BOLTS, NUTS, SCREWS, RIVETS & WASHERS
3460	6	METAL FORGINGS & STAMPINGS
3470	6	COATING, ENGRAVING & ALLIED SERVICES
3480	6	ORDNANCE & ACCESSORIES (NO VEHICLES/GUIDED MISSILES)

3490	6	MISCELLANEOUS FABRICATED METAL PRODUCTS
3510	10	ENGINES & TURBINES
3523	10	FARM MACHINERY & EQUIPMENT
3524	10	LAWN & GARDEN TRACTORS & HOME LAWN & GARDEN EQUIP
3530	10	CONSTRUCTION, MINING & MATERIALS HANDLING MACHINERY & EQUIP
3531	10	CONSTRUCTION MACHINERY & EQUIP
3532	10	MINING MACHINERY & EQUIP (NO OIL & GAS FIELD MACH & EQUIP)
3533	4	OIL & GAS FIELD MACHINERY & EQUIPMENT
3537	10	INDUSTRIAL TRUCKS, TRACTORS, TRAILERS & STACKERS
3540	10	METALWORKG MACHINERY & EQUIPMENT
3541	10	MACHINE TOOLS, METAL CUTTING TYPES
3550	10	SPECIAL INDUSTRY MACHINERY (NO METALWORKING MACHINERY)
3555	10	PRINTING TRADES MACHINERY & EQUIPMENT
3559	10	SPECIAL INDUSTRY MACHINERY, NEC
3560	10	GENERAL INDUSTRIAL MACHINERY & EQUIPMENT
3561	10	PUMPS & PUMPING EQUIPMENT
3562	6	BALL & ROLLER BEARINGS
3564	6	INDUSTRIAL & COMMERCIAL FANS & BLOWERS & AIR PURIFING EQUIP
3567	6	INDUSTRIAL PROCESS FURNACES & OVENS
3569	6	GENERAL INDUSTRIAL MACHINERY & EQUIPMENT, NEC

3570	3	COMPUTER & OFFICE EQUIPMENT
3571	3	ELECTRONIC COMPUTERS
3572	3	COMPUTER STORAGE DEVICES
3575	3	COMPUTER TERMINALS
3576	3	COMPUTER COMMUNICATIONS EQUIPMENT
3577	3	COMPUTER PERIPHERAL EQUIPMENT, NEC
3578	3	CALCULATING & ACCOUNTING MACHINES (NO ELECTRONIC COMPUTERS)
3579	3	OFFICE MACHINES, NEC
3580	6	REFRIGERATION & SERVICE INDUSTRY MACHINERY
3585	6	AIR-COND & WARM AIR HEATG EQUIP & COMM & INDL REFRIG EQUIP
3590	6	MISC INDUSTRIAL & COMMERCIAL MACHINERY & EQUIPMENT
3600	10	ELECTRONIC & OTHER ELECTRICAL EQUIPMENT (NO COMPUTER EQUIP)
3612	10	POWER, DISTRIBUTION & SPECIALTY TRANSFORMERS
3613	10	SWITCHGEAR & SWITCHBOARD APPARATUS
3620	10	ELECTRICAL INDUSTRIAL APPARATUS
3621	10	MOTORS & GENERATORS
3630	11	HOUSEHOLD APPLIANCES
3634	11	ELECTRIC HOUSEWARES & FANS
3640	11	ELECTRIC LIGHTING & WIRING EQUIPMENT
3651	11	HOUSEHOLD AUDIO & VIDEO EQUIPMENT
3652	11	PHONOGRAPH RECORDS & PRERECORDED AUDIO TAPES & DISKS
3661	11	TELEPHONE & TELEGRAPH APPARATUS

3663	11	RADIO & TV BROADCASTING & COMMUNICATIONS EQUIPMENT
3669	11	COMMUNICATIONS EQUIPMENT, NEC
3670	10	ELECTRONIC COMPONENTS & ACCESSORIES
3672	3	PRINTED CIRCUIT BOARDS
3674	10	SEMICONDUCTORS & RELATED DEVICES
3677	10	ELECTRONIC COILS, TRANSFORMERS & OTHER INDUCTORS
3678	10	ELECTRONIC CONNECTORS
3679	10	ELECTRONIC COMPONENTS, NEC
3690	10	MISCELLANEOUS ELECTRICAL MACHINERY, EQUIPMENT & SUPPLIES
3695	11	MAGNETIC & OPTICAL RECORDING MEDIA
3711	5	MOTOR VEHICLES & PASSENGER CAR BODIES
3713	5	TRUCK & BUS BODIES
3714	5	MOTOR VEHICLE PARTS & ACCESSORIES
3715	5	TRUCK TRAILERS
3716	5	MOTOR HOMES
3720	5	AIRCRAFT & PARTS
3721	5	AIRCRAFT
3724	5	AIRCRAFT ENGINES & ENGINE PARTS
3728	5	AIRCRAFT PARTS & AUXILIARY EQUIPMENT, NEC
3730	5	SHIP & BOAT BUILDING & REPAIRING
3743	5	RAILROAD EQUIPMENT
3751	5	MOTORCYCLES, BICYCLES & PARTS
3760	5	GUIDED MISSILES & SPACE VEHICLES & PARTS

3790	5	MISCELLANEOUS TRANSPORTATION EQUIPMENT
3812	5	SEARCH, DETECTION, NAVAGATION, GUIDANCE, AERONAUTICAL SYS
3821	10	LABORATORY APPARATUS & FURNITURE
3822	10	AUTO CONTROLS FOR REGULATING RESIDENTIAL & COMML ENVIRONMENTS
3823	10	INDUSTRIAL INSTRUMENTS FOR MEASUREMENT, DISPLAY, AND CONTROL
3824	10	TOTALIZING FLUID METERS & COUNTING DEVICES
3825	10	INSTRUMENTS FOR MEAS & TESTING OF ELECTRICITY & ELEC SIGNALS
3826	10	LABORATORY ANALYTICAL INSTRUMENTS
3827	10	OPTICAL INSTRUMENTS & LENSES
3829	10	MEASURING & CONTROLLING DEVICES, NEC
3841	10	SURGICAL & MEDICAL INSTRUMENTS & APPARATUS
3842	10	ORTHOPEDIC, PROSTHETIC & SURGICAL APPLIANCES & SUPPLIES
3843	10	DENTAL EQUIPMENT & SUPPLIES
3844	10	X-RAY APPARATUS & TUBES & RELATED IRRADIATION APPARATUS
3845	10	ELECTROMEDICAL & ELECTROTHERAPEUTIC APPARATUS
3851	10	OPHTHALMIC GOODS
3861	10	PHOTOGRAPHIC EQUIPMENT & SUPPLIES
3873	2	WATCHES, CLOCKS, CLOCKWORK OPERATED DEVICES/PARTS
3910	2	JEWELRY, SILVERWARE & PLATED WARE

3911	2	JEWELRY, PRECIOUS METAL
3931	5	MUSICAL INSTRUMENTS
3942	5	DOLLS & STUFFED TOYS
3944	5	GAMES, TOYS & CHILDREN'S VEHICLES (NO DOLLS & BICYCLES)
3949	5	SPORTING & ATHLETIC GOODS, NEC
3950	9	PENS, PENCILS & OTHER ARTISTS' MATERIALS
3960	6	COSTUME JEWELRY & NOVELTIES
3990	6	MISCELLANEOUS MANUFACTURING INDUSTRIES
4011	5	RAILROADS, LINE-HAUL OPERATING
4013	5	RAILROAD SWITCHING & TERMINAL ESTABLISHMENTS
4100	5	LOCAL & SUBURBAN TRANSIT & INTERURBAN HWY PASSENGER TRANS
4210	5	TRUCKING & COURIER SERVICES (NO AIR)
4213	5	TRUCKING (NO LOCAL)
4220	5	PUBLIC WAREHOUSING & STORAGE
4231	5	TERMINAL MAINTENANCE FACILITIES FOR MOTOR FREIGHT TRANSPORT
4400	5	WATER TRANSPORTATION
4412	5	DEEP SEA FOREIGN TRANSPORTATION OF FREIGHT
4512	5	AIR TRANSPORTATION, SCHEDULED
4513	5	AIR COURIER SERVICES
4522	5	AIR TRANSPORTATION, NONSCHEDULED
4581	5	AIRPORTS, FLYING FIELDS & AIRPORT TERMINAL SERVICES
4610	4	PIPELINES (NO NATURAL GAS)

4700	5	TRANSPORTATION SERVICES
4731	5	ARRANGEMENT OF TRANSPORTATION OF FREIGHT & CARGO
4812	11	RADIOTELEPHONE COMMUNICATIONS
4813	11	TELEPHONE COMMUNICATIONS (NO RADIOTELEPHONE)
4822	11	TELEGRAPH & OTHER MESSAGE COMMUNICATIONS
4832	11	RADIO BROADCASTING STATIONS
4833	11	TELEVISION BROADCASTING STATIONS
4841	11	CABLE & OTHER PAY TELEVISION SERVICES
4899	11	COMMUNICATIONS SERVICES, NEC
4900	2	ELECTRIC, GAS & SANITARY SERVICES
4911	2	ELECTRIC SERVICES
4922	2	NATURAL GAS TRANSMISSION
4923	2	NATURAL GAS TRANSMISSION & DISTRIBUTION
4924	2	NATURAL GAS DISTRIBUTION
4931	2	ELECTRIC & OTHER SERVICES COMBINED
4932	2	GAS & OTHER SERVICES COMBINED
4941	2	WATER SUPPLY
4950	6	SANITARY SERVICES
4953	6	REFUSE SYSTEMS
4955	6	HAZARDOUS WASTE MANAGEMENT
4961	2	STEAM & AIR-CONDITIONING SUPPLY
4991	2	COGENERATION SERVICES & SMALL POWER PRODUCERS
5000	2	WHOLESALE—DURABLE GOODS

5010	5	WHOLESALE—MOTOR VEHICLES & MOTOR VEHICLE PARTS & SUPPLIES
5013	5	WHOLESALE—MOTOR VEHICLE SUPPLIES & NEW PARTS
5020	2	WHOLESALE—FURNITURE & HOME FURNISHINGS
5030	6	WHOLESALE—LUMBER & OTHER CONSTRUCTION MATERIALS
5031	6	WHOLESALE—LUMBER, PLYWOOD, MILLWORK & WOOD PANELS
5040	2	WHOLESALE—PROFESSIONAL & COMMERCIAL EQUIPMENT & SUPPLIES
5045	3	WHOLESALE—COMPUTERS & PERIPHERAL EQUIPMENT & SOFTWARE
5047	9	WHOLESALE—MEDICAL, DENTAL & HOSPITAL EQUIPMENT & SUPPLIES
5050	5	WHOLESALE—METALS & MINERALS (NO PETROLEUM)
5051	5	WHOLESALE—METALS SERVICE CENTERS & OFFICES
5063	10	WHOLESALE—ELECTRICAL APPARATUS & EQUIPMENT, WIRING SUPPLIES
5064	10	WHOLESALE—ELECTRICAL APPLIANCES, TV & RADIO SETS
5065	10	WHOLESALE—ELECTRONIC PARTS & EQUIPMENT, NEC
5070	6	WHOLESALE—HARDWARE & PLUMBING & HEATING EQUIPMENT & SUPPLIES
5072	6	WHOLESALE—HARDWARE
5080	6	WHOLESALE—MACHINERY, EQUIPMENT & SUPPLIES
5082	6	WHOLESALE—CONSTRUCTION & MINING (NO PETRO) MACHINERY & EQUIP

5084	6	WHOLESALE—INDUSTRIAL MACHINERY & EQUIPMENT
5090	2	WHOLESALE—MISC DURABLE GOODS
5094	2	WHOLESALE—JEWELRY, WATCHES, PRECIOUS STONES & METALS
5099	2	WHOLESALE—DURABLE GOODS, NEC
5110	9	WHOLESALE—PAPER & PAPER PRODUCTS
5122	9	WHOLESALE—DRUGS, PROPRIETARIES & DRUGGISTS' SUNDRIES
5130	9	WHOLESALE—APPAREL, PIECE GOODS & NOTIONS
5140	2	WHOLESALE—GROCERIES & RELATED PRODUCTS
5141	2	WHOLESALE—GROCERIES, GENERAL LINE
5150	5	WHOLESALE—FARM PRODUCT RAW MATERIALS
5160	6	WHOLESALE—CHEMICALS & ALLIED PRODUCTS
5171	4	WHOLESALE—PETROLEUM BULK STATIONS & TERMINALS
5172	4	WHOLESALE—PETROLEUM & PETROLEUM PRODUCTS (NO BULK STATIONS)
5180	9	WHOLESALE—BEER, WINE & DISTILLED ALCOHOLIC BEVERAGES
5190	2	WHOLESALE—MISCELLANEOUS NONDURABLE GOODS
5200	6	RETAIL—BUILDING MATERIALS, HARDWARE, GARDEN SUPPLY
5211	6	RETAIL—LUMBER & OTHER BUILDING MATERIALS DEALERS
5271	2	RETAIL—MOBILE HOME DEALERS
5311	2	RETAIL—DEPARTMENT STORES

5331	2	RETAIL—VARIETY STORES
5399	2	RETAIL—MISC GENERAL MERCHANDISE STORES
5400	2	RETAIL—FOOD STORES
5411	2	RETAIL—GROCERY STORES
5412	2	RETAIL—CONVENIENCE STORES
5500	2	RETAIL—AUTO DEALERS & GASOLINE STATIONS
5531	2	RETAIL—AUTO & HOME SUPPLY STORES
5600	9	RETAIL—APPAREL & ACCESSORY STORES
5621	9	RETAIL—WOMEN'S CLOTHING STORES
5651	9	RETAIL—FAMILY CLOTHING STORES
5661	9	RETAIL—SHOE STORES
5700	2	RETAIL—HOME FURNITURE, FURNISHINGS & EQUIPMENT STORES
5712	2	RETAIL—FURNITURE STORES
5731	2	RETAIL—RADIO, TV & CONSUMER ELECTRONICS STORES
5734	2	RETAIL—COMPUTER & COMPUTER SOFTWARE STORES
5735	2	RETAIL—RECORD & PRERECORDED TAPE STORES
5810	5	RETAIL—EATING & DRINKING PLACES
5812	5	RETAIL—EATING PLACES
5900	2	RETAIL—MISCELLANEOUS RETAIL
5912	1	RETAIL—DRUG STORES AND PROPRIETARY STORES
5940	2	RETAIL—MISCELLANEOUS SHOPPING GOODS STORES
5944	2	RETAIL—JEWELRY STORES

5945	2	RETAIL—HOBBY, TOY & GAME SHOPS
5960	2	RETAIL—NONSTORE RETAILERS
5961	2	RETAIL—CATALOG & MAIL-ORDER HOUSES
5990	2	RETAIL—RETAIL STORES, NEC
6021	7	NATIONAL COMMERCIAL BANKS
6022	7	STATE COMMERCIAL BANKS
6029	7	COMMERCIAL BANKS, NEC
6035	7	SAVINGS INSTITUTION, FEDERALLY CHARTERED
6036	7	SAVINGS INSTITUTIONS, NOT FEDERALLY CHARTERED
6099	7	FUNCTIONS RELATED TO DEPOSITORY BANKING, NEC
6111	7	FEDERAL & FEDERALLY SPONSORED CREDIT AGENCIES
6141	7	PERSONAL CREDIT INSTITUTIONS
6153	7	SHORT-TERM BUSINESS CREDIT INSTITUTIONS
6159	7	MISCELLANEOUS BUSINESS CREDIT INSTITUTIONS
6162	7	MORTGAGE BANKERS & LOAN CORRESPONDENTS
6163	7	LOAN BROKERS
6172	7	FINANCE LESSORS
6189	5	ASSET-BACKED SECURITIES
6199	7	FINANCE SERVICES
6200	8	SECURITY & COMMODITY BROKERS, DEALERS, EXCHANGES & SERVICES
6211	8	SECURITY BROKERS, DEALERS & FLOTATION COMPANIES

6221	8	COMMODITY CONTRACTS BROKERS & DEALERS
6282	6	INVESTMENT ADVICE
6311	1	LIFE INSURANCE
6321	1	ACCIDENT & HEALTH INSURANCE
6324	1	HOSPITAL & MEDICAL SERVICE PLANS
6331	1	FIRE, MARINE & CASUALTY INSURANCE
6351	1	SURETY INSURANCE
6361	1	TITLE INSURANCE
6399	1	INSURANCE CARRIERS, NEC
6411	1	INSURANCE AGENTS, BROKERS & SERVICE
6500	8	REAL ESTATE
6510	8	REAL ESTATE OPERATORS (NO DEVELOPERS) & LESSORS
6512	8	OPERATORS OF NONRESIDENTIAL BUILDINGS
6513	8	OPERATORS OF APARTMENT BUILDINGS
6519	8	LESSORS OF REAL PROPERTY, NEC
6531	8	REAL ESTATE AGENTS & MANAGERS (FOR OTHERS)
6532	8	REAL ESTATE DEALERS (FOR THEIR OWN ACCOUNT)
6552	8	LAND SUBDIVIDERS & DEVELOPERS (NO CEMETERIES)
6770	9	BLANK CHECKS
6792	4	OIL ROYALTY TRADERS
6794	3	PATENT OWNERS & LESSORS
6795	4	MINERAL ROYALTY TRADERS
6798	8	REAL ESTATE INVESTMENT TRUSTS

6799	8	INVESTORS, NEC
7000	8	HOTELS, ROOMING HOUSES, CAMPS & OTHER LODGING PLACES
7011	8	HOTELS & MOTELS
7200	11	SERVICES—PERSONAL SERVICES
7310	11	SERVICES—ADVERTISING
7311	11	SERVICES—ADVERTISING AGENCIES
7320	11	SERVICES—CONSUMER CREDIT REPORTING, COLLECTION AGENCIES
7330	11	SERVICES—MAILING, REPRODUCTION, COMMERCIAL ART & PHOTOGRAPHY
7331	11	SERVICES—DIRECT MAIL ADVERTISING SERVICES
7340	8	SERVICES—TO DWELLINGS & OTHER BUILDINGS
7350	6	SERVICES—MISCELLANEOUS EQUIPMENT RENTAL & LEASING
7359	6	SERVICES—EQUIPMENT RENTAL & LEASING, NEC
7361	8	SERVICES—EMPLOYMENT AGENCIES
7363	11	SERVICES—HELP SUPPLY SERVICES
7370	3	SERVICES—COMPUTER PROGRAMMING, DATA PROCESSING, ETC.
7371	3	SERVICES—COMPUTER PROGRAMMING SERVICES
7372	3	SERVICES—PREPACKAGED SOFTWARE
7373	3	SERVICES—COMPUTER INTEGRATED SYSTEMS DESIGN
7374	3	SERVICES—COMPUTER PROCESSING & DATA PREPARATION

7377	3	SERVICES—COMPUTER RENTAL & LEASING
7380	11	SERVICES—MISCELLANEOUS BUSINESS SERVICES
7381	11	SERVICES—DETECTIVE, GUARD & ARMORED CAR SERVICES
7384	11	SERVICES—PHOTOFINISHING LABORATORIES
7385	11	SERVICES—TELEPHONE INTERCONNECT SYSTEMS
7389	2 & 3	SERVICES—BUSINESS SERVICES, NEC
7500	5	SERVICES—AUTOMOTIVE REPAIR, SERVICES & PARKING
7510	5	SERVICES—AUTO RENTAL & LEASING (NO DRIVERS)
7600	11	SERVICES—MISCELLANEOUS REPAIR SERVICES
7812	5	SERVICES—MOTION PICTURE & VIDEO TAPE PRODUCTION
7819	5	SERVICES—ALLIED TO MOTION PICTURE PRODUCTION
7822	5	SERVICES—MOTION PICTURE & VIDEO TAPE DISTRIBUTION
7829	5	SERVICES—ALLIED TO MOTION PICTURE DISTRIBUTION
7830	5	SERVICES—MOTION PICTURE THEATERS
7841	5	SERVICES—VIDEO TAPE RENTAL
7900	5	SERVICES—AMUSEMENT & RECREATION SERVICES
7948	5	SERVICES—RACING, INCLUDING TRACK OPERATION
7990	5	SERVICES—MISCELLANEOUS AMUSEMENT & RECREATION

7997	5	SERVICES—MEMBERSHIP SPORTS & RECREATION CLUBS
8000	9	SERVICES—HEALTH SERVICES
8011	1	SERVICES—OFFICES & CLINICS OF DOCTORS OF MEDICINE
8050	11	SERVICES—NURSING & PERSONAL CARE FACILITIES
8051	11	SERVICES—SKILLED NURSING CARE FACILITIES
8060	1	SERVICES—IIOSPITALS
8062	1	SERVICES—GENERAL MEDICAL & SURGICAL HOSPITALS, NEC
8071	9	SERVICES—MEDICAL LABORATORIES
8082	9	SERVICES—HOME HEALTH CARE SERVICES
8090	9	SERVICES—MISC HEALTH & ALLIED SERVICES, NEC
8093	1	SERVICES—SPECIALTY OUTPATIENT FACILITIES, NEC
8111	11	SERVICES—LEGAL SERVICES
8200	11	SERVICES—EDUCATIONAL SERVICES
8300	9	SERVICES—SOCIAL SERVICES
8351	9	SERVICES—CHILD DAY CARE SERVICES
8600	5	SERVICES—MEMBERSHIP ORGANIZATIONS
8700	6	SERVICES—ENGINEERING, ACCOUNTING, RESEARCH, MANAGEMENT
8711	6	SERVICES—ENGINEERING SERVICES
8731	1	SERVICES—COMMERCIAL PHYSICAL & BIOLOGICAL RESEARCH
8734	9	SERVICES—TESTING LABORATORIES

8741	8	SERVICES—MANAGEMENT SERVICES
8742	8	SERVICES—MANAGEMENT CONSULTING SERVICES
8744	6	SERVICES—FACILITIES SUPPORT MANAGEMENT SERVICES
8880	99	AMERICAN DEPOSITARY RECEIPTS
8888	99	FOREIGN GOVERNMENTS
8900	11	SERVICES—SERVICES, NEC
9721	99	INTERNATIONAL AFFAIRS
9995	9	NONOPERATING ESTABLISHMENTS

CHAPTER 5

Skills
That Sell

> *"Knowing others is wisdom; knowing yourself is enlightenment."*
>
> —Lao-Tsu

Knowing your skills builds a rock-solid foundation for your Q statements. It will also be an extremely valuable lesson to you for interviewing.

If you know *as few as six* of your skills as well as you know your own home address, both your interview and your résumé are likely to be smashing successes. Once you can describe your skills (how you used them and what the result was) on your résumé and in your interview, you are literally unstoppable as a job seeker.

This is exactly what Q statements do. Consider this study:

When more than 4,000 employers were interviewed about why they did *not* select certain candidates, the first thing they said was that the candidates could not clearly describe their skills.

Now stop and read that last sentence again. It doesn't say that the candidates who were not chosen did not *have* the right skills for the job. It says that, in the employer's eyes, they *could not clearly describe their skills*. The employers in that survey also responded that, in their opinion, 85 percent of the job seekers they saw could not or would not describe their skills in a clear and specific manner.

You *will* be able to do this. And you certainly don't have to be a writer or a scholar to do so. All you have to know, you're going to learn in the next two chapters. If you know what the words *who, what, when, where, how,* and *why* and the question *what happened?* mean, you will very shortly become an expert at clearly describing your skills.

- Can you believe that simply by completing this and the next chapter, you will be part of the top 15 percent of job seekers? Well it's true. And the sad part is that everyone doesn't take the time or have the knowledge that *you* are going to learn in just a few pages. Are you ready?

Three Categories of Skills

There are three types of skills that we will be talking about in this chapter, and all of them are very important for both your résumé and your interview.

These three essential skill categories are

1. General skills
2. Job-specific skills
3. Personal traits or characteristics

- Identifying your skills in each of these three categories is the first step in crafting Q statements clearly and convincingly on your résumé.

General Skills

First, let's take a look at general skills and see why they can be so important to you, whether you're planning to stay in the same occupation or are thinking about making a move into an entirely new profession.

Here are some examples of general skills to remind you of some of the actions you may have performed in the past while on the job, volunteering, going to school, or in other situations. Please go through the list and check off the skills that you know how to perform and even the ones that you feel you *could* perform with just a little bit of practice.

- In other words, you don't have to be an expert at a skill to check it off on this list. You may have used the skill only once, but if you have even a bit of knowledge about how to use it, check it off.

After all, every time you switch to a new job, you have to brush up on or even spend a bit of time relearning certain skills. Be generous with yourself as you do this assessment. Don't cheat yourself out of a skill just because you feel you can't do it perfectly. Even experts aren't perfect.

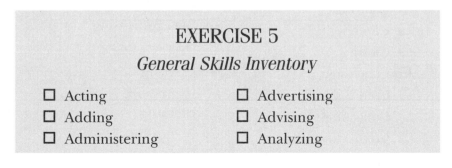

EXERCISE 5
General Skills Inventory

☐ Acting   ☐ Advertising
☐ Adding   ☐ Advising
☐ Administering   ☐ Analyzing

☐ Announcing
☐ Arranging
☐ Assessing
☐ Assisting
☐ Attaching
☐ Attending
☐ Auditing
☐ Balancing
☐ Budgeting
☐ Building chemical compounds
☐ Building cooperation
☐ Building rapport
☐ Building relationships
☐ Building structures
☐ Buying
☐ Calculating
☐ Caring
☐ Celebrating
☐ Charting
☐ Chiseling
☐ Choosing
☐ Classifying clients
☐ Cleaning
☐ Clearing
☐ Climbing
☐ Closing
☐ Coaching
☐ Cold calling
☐ Collecting
☐ Communicating feelings

☐ Communicating ideas
☐ Communicating instructions or commands
☐ Communicating in writing
☐ Communicating nonverbally
☐ Communicating verbally
☐ Competing
☐ Compiling
☐ Completing
☐ Composing
☐ Conceptualizing
☐ Consulting
☐ Convening
☐ Cooperating
☐ Coordinating
☐ Correcting
☐ Corresponding
☐ Counseling
☐ Crafting
☐ Creating
☐ Customer relations
☐ Dancing
☐ Data processing
☐ Decision making
☐ Decorating
☐ Decreasing
☐ Defining
☐ Delegating
☐ Designing

☐ Developing
☐ Diagnosing
☐ Directing
☐ Diving
☐ Drafting
☐ Drawing
☐ Dressing
☐ Driving
☐ Editing
☐ Educating
☐ Elevating
☐ Eliminating
☐ E-mail
☐ Empathizing
☐ Enforcing
☐ Engineering
☐ Entertaining
☐ Enumerating
☐ Evaluating
☐ Fighting
☐ Filing
☐ Financial
☐ Financing
☐ Finding
☐ Finishing
☐ Fixing
☐ Flying
☐ Forecasting
☐ Framing
☐ Fund-raising
☐ Gardening

☐ Gesturing
☐ Gifting
☐ Giving
☐ Grafting
☐ Graphing
☐ Greeting
☐ Growing
☐ Guarding
☐ Handling
☐ Healing
☐ Helping
☐ Hiring
☐ Illustrating
☐ Imaging
☐ Imagining
☐ Imbuing
☐ Implementing
☐ Increasing
☐ Influencing
☐ Initiating into a tank
☐ Injecting
☐ Innovating
☐ Integrating
☐ Intervening
☐ Inventing
☐ Investing
☐ Judging
☐ Launching
☐ Leading
☐ Lecturing
☐ Lifting

☐ Lighting
☐ Listening
☐ Litigating
☐ Locating
☐ Lowering
☐ Maintaining
☐ Managing
☐ Marketing
☐ Massaging
☐ Mediating
☐ Mentoring
☐ Mitigating
☐ Molding
☐ Monitoring
☐ Mounting
☐ Multiplying
☐ Networking
☐ New rising
☐ Nullifying
☐ Numbering
☐ Nursing
☐ Nurturing
☐ Observing
☐ Operating
☐ Orchestrating
☐ Organizing
☐ Orienting
☐ Overseeing
☐ Painting
☐ Performing
☐ Persuading
☐ Piloting

☐ Planning
☐ Playing
☐ Polishing
☐ Prescribing
☐ Presenting
☐ Preserving
☐ Preventing
☐ Probing
☐ Producing
☐ Program managing
☐ Programming
☐ Programming computers
☐ Project managing
☐ Promoting
☐ Prospecting
☐ Public speaking
☐ Publishing
☐ Qualifying
☐ Quality assurance
☐ Quantifying
☐ Raising
☐ Rebuilding
☐ Reconciling
☐ Reconstructing
☐ Recording
☐ Redirecting
☐ Redoing
☐ Refurbishing
☐ Renovating
☐ Repairing
☐ Reporting
☐ Researching

☐ Responding	☐ Team building
☐ Retracting	☐ Teasing
☐ Returning	☐ Telecommunicating
☐ Revamping	☐ Telemarketing
☐ Reversing	☐ Telephoning
☐ Sales	☐ Tending
☐ Sanding	☐ Terminating
☐ Sanitizing	☐ Tipping
☐ Saving	☐ Titling
☐ Scaling	☐ Tooling
☐ Sealing	☐ Training
☐ Searching	☐ Translating
☐ Selecting	☐ Transporting
☐ Selling	☐ Treading
☐ Servicing	☐ Treating
☐ Serving	☐ Tripling
☐ Sewing	☐ Troubleshooting
☐ Signaling	☐ Ultrasound
☐ Signing	☐ Understanding
☐ Sizing	☐ Unplugging
☐ Speaking	☐ Using
☐ Stocking	☐ Using equipment
☐ Stripping	☐ Using the Internet
☐ Structuring	☐ Using resources
☐ Supervising	☐ Watching
☐ Supporting	☐ Weaving
☐ Surveying	☐ Welding
☐ Synchronizing	☐ Winning
☐ Synergizing	☐ Wiring
☐ Taking	☐ Wrangling
☐ Talking	☐ Writing
☐ Teaching	☐ X-ray

Write other general skills or action words that are not on this list, but that fit you or your past jobs:

_____

_____

_____

_____

_____

_____

_____

_____

_____

At this point, you should be feeling pretty good. I will bet you right now that you actually have more skills than you suspected you had.

You may also be thinking, "Okay, good organizational skills, communication abilities, and supervisory accomplishments are all parts of my profile, but that's not *all* there is to what I know how to do."

You're absolutely right!

Job-Specific Skills

All we've talked about so far are very general skills that could be used in a number of jobs. But when you think about it, in your *particular* area of expertise, you use very specific skills that are not used in other professions.

We call these abilities job-specific skills, or those abilities that you need if you are to succeed in your particular job at your particular company in your particular industry.

Scan the following information for some examples of job-specific skills for different occupations. You may not see your occupation listed, but you'll get an idea of the difference between job-specific skills and the general skills you've already identified.

- Your job-specific skills are usually listed on your résumé, but remember to describe exactly *what you did* with those skills, as we will in the next chapter with Q statements.

Please take a look now at the following lists of some job-specific skills. These are abilities in which proficiency is necessary in selected occupations.

For example, people in accounting, bookkeeping or finance may have the following job-specific skills:

- Accounts payable
- Accounts receivable
- Payroll
- Tax filings

A football player would have

- An understanding of football strategy
- The ability to stay in shape off-season
- The ability to play the position to which he is assigned
- Knowledge of how to get motivated before the game.

A computer programmer's job-specific skills would include knowledge of

- Computer languages
- Computer platforms
- Computer programs
- Computer networking

A surgeon would have expert knowledge of

- Human anatomy and physiology
- How to make a diagnosis and prognosis
- Necessary sterilization procedures
- The ability to perform surgery

Marketing specialists have job-specific skills like

- Press release writing
- Trade show coordinating
- Forecasting
- Branding

Psychotherapists would have special skills in

- Diagnosing a client's mental health
- Nonverbal behavior
- Cognitive behavioral therapy
- Brief therapy

A financial planner may possess

- Special licenses, like a Series 7 or a Series 35
- Knowledge of stocks, bonds, insurance, and mutual funds
- Information concerning advising clients on how to save money
- Knowledge of retirement planning

An environmental planner would have job-specific skills such as

- Knowledge of geology
- Master of biology and chemistry
- Knowledge of city and county zoning laws
- Information on the causes of and solutions for pollution

A publisher would be required to have

- Exceptional literacy
- Expertise in the publishing process, from pitching to marketing
- Knowledge of how to evaluate books for publication
- Insight into trends in bookselling

Job-specific skills of a semiconductor assembler would be

- Knowledge of the component parts of a wafer
- Information on clean room technology
- Knowledge of safety procedures
- Superior fine motor control

An office manager would know how to

- Order office supplies and keep the whole office running within a budget
- Operate Microsoft Office or other computer programs
- Answer the phone, take messages, and route calls professionally
- Operate modern office equipment

Your job or career was very likely not mentioned in this section. Still, I think you've caught on quickly to the differences between general and job-specific skills and can now identify some job-specific skills of your own.

EXERCISE 6

Job-Specific Skills Inventory

Please write 10 to 20 job specific skills that you've acquired. Don't forget to include *both* the skills you've used in your work life *and* those you've used in other settings, such as the following:

- Running a household
- Being a student
- Contributing to your church, temple, or faith
- Being in a club
- Playing on a sports team
- Serving in the military

- Volunteering
- Being an intern
- Serving a jail sentence
- Traveling

Please write your job-specific skills here.

_____

_____

_____

_____

_____

_____

_____

_____

_____

Keep in mind that we are always learning and hopefully accepting new responsibilities, and thus even things that you may take for granted, such as doing your laundry, balancing your checkbook, replacing a flat tire, or investing in the stock market as a hobby, are all part of who you are and what you can do.

Just think of all the things you do in a day, a week, a year, or a decade! You could probably write a book about it, but don't worry. We're just going to stick to a one- or two-page résumé for now.

Personal Characteristics

Personal characteristics are not like the other skills you've just identified. Personal characteristics are not something that you *do*; they instead represent something that you *are*.

- Personal characteristics are special qualities that make up parts of your personality. Your personality greatly affects how you do your job and how well suited you would be for a certain job or company.

It's possible that you already know a typical personal profile for your industry or occupation. In that case, by all means list the qualities that make up that profile. But let's take it a bit further and include those characteristics that make you, and only you, a unique contributor to the workplace.

EXERCISE 7

Personal Characteristics Inventory

The following is a list (inventory) of many personal traits. My guess is that you possess quite a few of these qualities and that they will make a positive impact on both your résumé and your interview. Please place a check by those personal characteristics that apply to you.

Remember, there's nothing to be gained from being modest. If you asked any good friend or coworker, she would probably agree that you do indeed possess these qualities. *Be sure to give yourself credit for your own best traits.*

☐ Accepting   ☐ Assertive

☐ Accurate   ☐ Aware

☐ Achievement oriented   ☐ Balanced

☐ Action oriented   ☐ Brilliant

☐ Aggressive   ☐ Businesslike

☐ Ambitious   ☐ Calm

☐ Analytical   ☐ Caring

☐ Artistic   ☐ Cautious

☐ Challenging	☐ Fair
☐ Charismatic	☐ Fit
☐ Committed	☐ Friendly
☐ Communicative	☐ Frugal
☐ Compassionate	☐ Generous
☐ Competitive	☐ Gentle
☐ Concerned	☐ Genuine
☐ Confident	☐ Gifted
☐ Conservative	☐ Hardworking
☐ Courageous	☐ Healthy
☐ Creative	☐ Helpful
☐ Dedicated	☐ High self-esteem
☐ Dependable	☐ Honest
☐ Detail oriented	☐ Humorous
☐ Determined	☐ Independent
☐ Diligent	☐ Innovative
☐ Diplomatic	☐ Insightful
☐ Direct	☐ Inspirational
☐ Driven	☐ Intellectual
☐ Dynamic	☐ Intelligent
☐ Easygoing	☐ Introverted
☐ Economical	☐ Intuitive
☐ Effective	☐ Inventive
☐ Efficient	☐ Kind
☐ Emotionally strong	☐ Knowledgeable
☐ Energetic	☐ Likable
☐ Entertaining	☐ Lively
☐ Enthusiastic	☐ Logical
☐ Entrepreneurial	☐ Loved
☐ Ethical	☐ Loyal
☐ Exemplary	☐ Mature
☐ Expressive	☐ Methodical

☐ Meticulous
☐ Modest
☐ Moral
☐ Motivating
☐ Nice
☐ Nurturing
☐ Obedient
☐ Observant
☐ Optimistic
☐ Orderly
☐ Outgoing
☐ Patient
☐ Perfectionist
☐ Persuasive
☐ Physically strong
☐ Powerful
☐ Precise
☐ Private
☐ Proactive
☐ Productive
☐ Punctual
☐ Purposeful
☐ Rational
☐ Relaxed
☐ Reserved
☐ Resilient
☐ Resourceful
☐ Respected
☐ Respectful
☐ Responsible
☐ Responsive
☐ Results oriented

☐ Scientific
☐ Self-controlled
☐ Self-motivated
☐ Sincere
☐ Sociable
☐ Spontaneous
☐ Supportive
☐ Systematic
☐ Tactful
☐ Task oriented
☐ Team oriented
☐ Team player
☐ Tenacious
☐ Thorough
☐ Thoughtful
☐ Thrifty
☐ Tidy
☐ Tolerant
☐ Trustworthy
☐ Uninhibited
☐ Unique
☐ Unselfish
☐ Unstoppable
☐ Unusual
☐ Visionary
☐ Vivacious
☐ Warm
☐ Well groomed
☐ Well liked
☐ Well spoken
☐ Winner

Please write any other positive words that come to mind when describing yourself. Don't forget the compliments that *others* have given you.

_____

_____

_____

_____

_____

_____

_____

_____

_____

Excellent! Now that you've taken the time to really concentrate on the special skills and personal characteristics that you possess, let's note them down for future reference so that you can refer to them at a glance when writing your résumé or when preparing for an interview. Choosing the skills that you like most and that are most relevant for your future, I'd like you to assemble what I call your skills arsenal. You may not use every single one of these skills on the first résumé you write, but I can guarantee that your selections will come in handy any time you wish to compose or revise your Fearless Résumé.

Modify Your Power Proposition

Note: If you think that some of the words you include in the next exercise are more suited to the specialties section of your power proposition than the ones you selected when you first wrote it, then by all means go back and change your power proposition so that it has your most up-to-date reflection of your specialties (skills) and your personal characteristics.

General Skills Arsenal

Please select and write your top 10 general skills.

1. _____
2. _____
3. _____
4. _____
5. _____
6. _____
7. _____
8. _____
9. _____
10. _____

Job-Specific Skills Arsenal

Good work! Now think about your 6 to 10 most used job-specific skills and note them here, keeping in mind that you may be using many of them to describe skills on your Fearless Résumé that pertain to a job or new career goal. Please select at least 6 to 10.

1. _____
2. _____
3. _____
4. _____
5. _____
6. _____
7. _____
8. _____
9. _____
10. _____

Personal Characteristics Arsenal

You've now completed a fantastic list of what some human resources people call your "hard" skills. Now, let's look at the very important aspect that is also important in the workplace—your personal characteristics—sometimes called your "soft" skills. Use the previous exercise in this chapter to select three to six of the personal characteristics that you know you have and that you think would be useful for the next job you apply for, and note them here.

1. _____

2. _____

3. _____

4. _____

5. _____

6. _____

- I'm impressed! Never again will you have to fumble or guess about what your strengths and abilities really are. They're right here on paper, and you should take a moment to feel *very* proud of them.

Your Unique Blend of Skills

I am not trying to be nice when I say that you—yes, you!—are absolutely unique, and therefore *profoundly* special. I defy you to search the world for a person with your *exact* blend of general skills, job-specific skills, and personal traits. Whether you believe in a supreme being, are a staunch geneticist, or are a bit of both, I will tell you that there is *no one* like you. Your Fearless Résumé will make that evident.

CHAPTER 6

Make Your Job History Sizzle

> *"The road to happiness lies in two simple principles— find what interests you and that you can do and put your whole soul into it."*
>
> —John D. Rockefeller III

Can you picture yourself saddled with the task of reading up to 1,500 résumés for *one* job opening? Well, you can be sure that *someone* is in the middle of doing just that right now. Let's say that you are the hiring manager. Imagine that you've reached résumé 809 out of the 1,500 you're responsible for reviewing. You've got to admit that, up to now, you've gathered a couple of "maybes," but no one résumé has really struck an *emotional* chord with you.

Suddenly, holding number 809 in your hand, you get a feeling in your gut the second you lay eyes on it, and you are eager to read more. This (Fearless) résumé conjures up vivid and clear images in your mind of the writer doing detailed, engaging, or even colorful tasks.

Even better, these tasks have consequences. They could help you as a manager! They could help the company!

Would you keep reading that résumé? Would it put you in a different mood? Do you think you might be relieved, hopeful, and happy?

Do you think that, if the descriptions of this person and her skills were closely enough matched to both the job requirements and your own personal preferences, you might even want to *meet* this person?

If you were a hiring manager, you bet you would. Hiring managers aren't robots, you know. The person reading your résumé is a real person, just like you. Just as you don't want the drudgery of reading a lot of dull documents, neither does he.

That's where Q statements come in. Q statements are more than just phrases about your job duties. Instead, they are dynamic and often measurable sentences that give rich sensory information.

- Because a Q statement is so specific and detailed, it causes readers to form pictures in their minds of you doing tasks and reaching goals that spell out "*hire.*"

What Is a Q Statement?

A Q statement is a phrase or sentence that actively and vividly describes something that you have accomplished.

Most often, Q statements include

1. A *skill* or *skills* that you used to accomplish this.
2. Some description of either *how, what, when, where*, or *why* you achieved this accomplishment.
3. A *measurement* of some sort, such as a number of people, an amount of money, a percentage, or a number on a scale.
4. The *result* of what you did—for example, how you helped your company, clients, customers, or patients.

Here's a formula for writing a Q statement:

Skill + what you did (including the quantity—usually a number) + the result of what you did

Turning Skills into Q Statements

Let's take the skill *supervised* (which you may have already checked on your general skills exercise in the last chapter) and make it into a Q statement using this formula.

"Supervised [skill] a group of *10 people* on a sales training project lasting *60 days* [what you did, plus numbers to measure what you did], which resulted in the group *exceeding the sales quota for the year by 28 percent* [the result of what you did].

Here are some more Q statements:

✓ Answered [skill] 250 customer service calls per day [what you did, plus a number to measure what you did], resulting in an average of 97 new customers per week, making the company over $6,000 in new customer registration fees per month [the result of what you did].

✓ Configured [skill] two new servers on a wireless networking system [what you did, plus a number to measure what you did] that decreased downtime by 24 percent, saving the company over $12,800 per month [the result of what you did].

You can see that the following Q statements also include a skill word, what the person did, some form of numerical measurement, and a clear result.

- ✓ Planned a fund-raising event involving 350 people paying $1,000 apiece that generated a net profit of over $30,000.
- ✓ Targeted a new market for vending machines that resulted in approximately 1,900 new vending machine locations and a gross profit of $47,890 per month.
- ✓ Sold over 15 new corporate training accounts per quarter, earning the company over $770,000 in new accounts revenue per year.
- ✓ Handled over 300 customer calls per day and routed them to over 85 employees.
- ✓ Instituted and implemented a manufacturing process that increased profits by 47 percent in the fourth quarter.
- ✓ Maintained at an average caseload of 55 multicultural clients, only 3 percent of whom required hospitalization.
- ✓ Engineered a prototype that tolerated 18 percent more stress than its precursor.
- ✓ Oversaw landscape design of projects costing up to $450,000.
- ✓ Reduced overhead by 37 percent while increasing profitability by 17 percent per year.

Getting the Employer to Visualize

In every Q statement, there is a little "story" that may include all or just some of the elements of

Who
What
When
Where

How

Why

How much

As in any good story, you want your readers to both be able to clearly picture, in their minds, what you're tallking about *and* have an emotional reaction to what you're saying. Let's look at some comparisons between Q statements and phrases that indicate "regular" job duties.

Comparison of Q Statements and Job Duties

PAIR 1. SKILL WORD: LED

Job duty: Led a successful team.

Q statement: Led a team of 12 computer software engineers to develop a new program that resulted in $1.6 million in profits after the first year of its launch.

PAIR 2. SKILL WORD: (TO) RUN

Job duty: Ran an office.

Q statement: Ran and kept detailed records for a busy dental office seeing more than 45 patients per day.

PAIR 3. SKILL WORD: COACH

Job duty: Coached a sports team.

Q statement: Coached a basketball team, using mind-body visualization techniques, that went from number 32 in the state to number 1 in a period of one year.

Did the *first* statement (job duty) in each of the pairs cause you to have a strong sense of what the writer did or how she might contribute to your company? How about the second account (Q statement)?

If you were reading one résumé that was full of statements of job duties and another résumé that was replete with Q statements, which of the two people would you want to interview? Remember, both the first and second statements represent the same skill. Which is more believable? Which is more compelling? Why?

- I think I can guess that you'd agree that Q statements sizzle, while job duty statements are stale.

The magic of a Q statement is not only that it causes your reader to have a more vivid reaction. There's something much more exciting about a Q statement.

When your reader can clearly "see" or "feel" what you did in one of your past jobs, as you describe it with a quantified statement, she also unconsciously imagines you achieving something similar at *her* company!

Don't Force It

Don't worry. You don't have to force the employer to create images in his mind, and you don't have to be a writer, either. If you just supply *detailed* information, which sometimes can be done by using numbers, measurements, amounts, and percentages along with places, people, ideas, and things, the employer's brain will respond automatically.

Using Your Skills as a Starting Point

Since the first word in a Q statement is almost always a skill, you can use some of the general skills and job-specific skills you selected in the last chapter to form some Q statements of your own. In the following statements, simply look at how the skill word fits into the Q statement. Just a bit later in the chapter, you'll find out how to quantify parts of your statement and/or show a quantified result of what you did.

Examples of Skill-Based Q Statements

SKILL: DRIVING

Statement: *Drove* over 350 miles per week through the Central Coast, delivering over 1 ton of cargo.

SKILL: LEADING

Statement: *Led* a team that produced a piston that was over 12 percent more effective than the previous version.

SKILL: SELLING

Statement: *Sold* an average of two real estate properties per month, totaling an average of $30,000 a month in commission.

SKILL: WINNING

Statement: *Won* an award in 2006 for decreasing materials costs from 871 per inch to 686 per inch.

SKILLS: INITIATING AND DEVELOPING

Statement: *Initiated* and *developed* a retraining program for the Hallerite County Police Department that improved public perception of police officers from 2.9 to 4.8 on a scale of 1 to 5.

SKILL: DESIGNED

Statement: *Designed* a new production process that decreased production time by four days a month, resulting in a savings of $430,000 quarterly.

You'll notice that the results and descriptions contained in a quantified statement almost always include some measurement, like a number, an amount of money, a percentage, or a number on a scale.

What we know about employers is that when you can show that you can increase certain things and/or decrease other things, you either directly or indirectly help the employer to *make a profit*.

- What could possibly be a more irresistible hook for an employer than making money?

How to Hook the Employer with a Q Statement

In general, you can be sure that when you directly or indirectly *increase* something that an employer wants, like one of the things listed here, you provide a tangible hook that makes him want to read more and ultimately can lead to an interview. Some things that you might show that you *increased* are

✓ Employee morale
✓ Prestige
✓ Safety
✓ Speed of production (saving time)
✓ Profits
✓ New products
✓ New services
✓ Good public perception
✓ Efficiency or integrity of operations
✓ Government compliance
✓ Branding
✓ Customers/clients
✓ Return on investment
✓ Overtaking competitors
✓ Expansion into new markets
✓ Locations
✓ Financial stability

The same thing is true in the other direction. When you *decrease* something that an employer doesn't want, it often can mean saving the employer money or the firm's reputation. Things that you can create hooks with your Q statements by *decreasing* are

✓ Waste
✓ Accidents
✓ Bad publicity
✓ Unlawful activities
✓ Inefficiency
✓ Downtime
✓ Overhead
✓ Expenses
✓ Workplace harassment
✓ Time it takes to complete a project or process

✓ Poor-quality products

✓ Returns

✓ Excessive maintenance

✓ Tardiness

✓ Sick days

✓ Lawsuits

✓ Disorganization

✓ Unacceptable health and safety practices

✓ (Usually) paying overtime

✓ Unattractive or dirty workplace

✓ Malfunction of equipment

Creating some Q statements right now will propel your résumé into the highest ranking and imbue your interview with the sound of earned success. Remember, you do not have to know *exact* numbers, percentages, or lengths of time.

- Sometimes it's just too hard to recall an exact number, so the best thing to do is to *estimate* your measurements and quanities to the best of your ability.

If you happen to have forgotten the exact details of some of your numbers—say that you indicated on your résumé that you earned $152,000 in sales, but the fact was that you really earned $149,934—no one, unless you're applying at an accounting firm, will call you a liar.

Most of us, of course, don't want to misrepresent ourselves; in fact, most of my clients actually *underestimate* their numbers on their résumés.

Please don't underestimate yourself. You must find a balance that's fair and honest. Few people can recall amounts to the point of perfection. When you are quantifying your accomplishments, just do your best to state your best guess, within reason, as to what you did or what results you achieved. One test for this is to ask, "Would I feel comfortable saying this figure out loud?" If you would, and you spare yourself the harsh judgment of perfectionism, your numbers are probably fine. If not, go back and adjust them a bit.

Now, please create at least five to ten Q statements for yourself. You may adjust them or use different ones when you actually compose your résumé, but there's nothing like getting into the habit of creating Q statements for your skills. It will make you believable, powerful, and, most of all, confident.

1. _____
   _____
   _____

2. _____
   _____
   _____

3. _____
   _____
   _____

4. _____
   _____
   _____

5. _____
   _____
   _____

6. _____
   _____
   _____

7. _____
   _____
   _____

8. _____

_____

_____

9. _____

_____

_____

10. _____

_____

_____

Good! In the next chapter, you'll see how well your Q statements fit into the body of your résumé in a section called "Employment History."

CHAPTER 7

Organize Your Data for Maximum Impact

"It is only when doing my work that I truly feel alive."

—Federico Fellini

Your Fearless Résumé, as a whole, can be seen as the answers to five simple questions that the employer wants to ask about you. They are

1. Who are you?
2. What do you want?
3. Tell me about yourself.
4. What can you do, and where and how have you done it? What was the result of your actions?
5. Where and how were you trained or educated?

That's it. Whether you're a carpenter, a nurse, or the vice president of a company, these five questions remain basically the same.

Résumé Blocks

Interestingly, in answering these five questions, there are also five mandatory sections of a Fearless Résumé (we'll refer to them as *blocks*). Here are the basic blocks of the résumé. They correspond exactly to the order of the questions just given.

1. The contact block (Who are you?)
2. The objective block (What do you want?)
3. The summary block (Tell me about yourself— your power proposition)
4. The employment history block (What can you do? Where have you done it? What were the results?— your Q statements)
5. The education and training block (Where were you educated?)

Résumés almost always start with block 1 (the contact block) and descend in order down the page to block 5 (the education and training block). That's it. It makes sense, doesn't it?

Order of Résumé Sections

The following is a working diagram of the order of each part of your Fearless Résumé, plus a guideline about the question each section answers.

Contact Block

Question: *Who are you?*
Answer: *Your name, address, phone number(s), and e-mail address*
Example:

Tom Collins
347 24th Avenue
Twin Peaks, WA 2733X
(555) 222-6767 Home
(555) 223-9375 Cell
tcollins@bestinternet.com

Objective Block

Question: *What do you want?*
Answer: *Your job objective (title of the job you're targeting)*
Example: A position as a senior accountant.

Summary Block

Question: *Tell me about yourself.*
Answer: *Your power proposition*
Summary: Over 5 years as an accountant in the health-care industry. Specialties include bookkeeping, accounts receivable, and payroll. Reduced accounts receivable time by an average of 6 days per month using QuickContact software, thereby saving the company over $3,200 in mailing costs. A.A. in Business; B.A. in Finance with an emphasis in Accounting.

Relevant (or "Technical") Skills Block [Optional]

Microsoft Office Suite	Bookkeeping	QuickBooks
Accounts payable	Accounts receivable	Payroll

Employment History Block

Question: *What can you do, and where have you done it? What were the results of your actions?*

Answer: *Your job title, the company(s) you worked for, the city and state, and the dates you were employed there (in that order)*

Plus two to six bulleted Q statements per job

Example:

Senior Accountant
Procorp Health Systems, Twin Peaks, WA   **1999–present**
(Use no less than two and no more than six Q statements)

✓ Q statement

✓ Q statement

✓ Q statement

✓ Q statement

✓ Q statement

✓ Q statement

Junior Accountant
Smindia Hospital, Smindia, WA   **1998–1999**

✓ Q statement

✓ Q statement

✓ Q statement

✓ Q statement

The following is the format if you have more than one job title at different times at the same company.

Jetlands Department Store
Bellingham, WA   **1995–1998**
Accountant I (1996–1998)

✓ Q statement

✓ Q statement

Customer Service Representative (1995–1996)

✓ Q statement

✓ Q statement

Education Block

Question: *Where were you educated or trained?*

Answer: *List your degrees, licenses, certificates, and any relevant education or training that is in progress.*

Example: Currently enrolled in a course of study leading to a Master of Business Administration with an emphasis in Finance at University of Seattle

B.A. Finance, University of Seattle

A.A. Accounting, Bellingham City College

Publications Block [Optional]

"The Impact of Government Provided Health Care on Acute Care Facilities Management," *Student Journal of Health Care Finance*, September 2006.

Awards Block [Optional]

Employee of the Year Award, Procorp Health Systems, 2001

Professional Affiliations Block [Optional]

Western U.S. Accounting Society

MBA Study Association of UOS

Here's another sample résumé with basic blocks that answers all five questions:

[Who are you?]

Lisa Y. Nguyen

26XX Hillsbury Court, FL 1XXXX

Home phone: (254) XXX-XX23

Mobile phone: (254) XXX-XX54

lisa_yvette_nguyen@hts.net

[What do you want?]

OBJECTIVE

A position as a production manager in the film industry.

[Tell me about yourself]

PROFESSIONAL SUMMARY

[*This section would contain Lisa's power proposition. You will notice that we don't actually write the words power proposition on the résumé itself. Instead, we identify this section on the résumé itself as "summary." Other words that are occasionally used instead of* summary *are* professional summary, highlights of qualifications, summary of qualifications, *and* professional expertise, *and you may feel free to use those terms on your résumé if you wish.*]

[What have you done, and with what result?]

WORK HISTORY

[*Your job title, the name of the company, its city and state, and the years that you worked there. We'll talk later about why you* do not *need to write the months that you worked, only the years. Your most recent job always goes first.*]

Production Manager
Sammy T. Productions, Tampa, FL   2005–2009

[*Underneath your title, years, and company, you'll write two to six Q statements.*]

- Managed a crew of 3 assistant directors, 4 production assistants, and production.
- Hired a technical and artistic crew of 349.
- Adhered to all Screen Actors Guild and IATSE union rules, including those for children.
- Negotiated and saved 18% of a $16 million budget.
- Scheduled a 27-day shooting schedule with 206 separate scenes.
- Collected records and analyzed personnel, equipment, and expendables usage throughout production to ensure staying on budget.

[*Continue in the same manner, going back only 10 to 15 years.*]

1st Assistant Director
Archway Film Visions, Orlando, FL   2003–2004

- Coordinated all action on set and ensured timely production of scenes, saving up to 30 minutes daily.
- Managed the actions of 2 other assistant directors and 1 set production assistant.
- Directed 8 second unit scenes and 14 special effects scenes.
- Assisted production manager in scheduling over 117 scenes.

2nd Assistant Director
Metro Net Pictures, Miami, FL   2002–2003

- Ensured that all 11 actors were dressed, made up, and ready for shooting scenes.
- Kept detailed daily records of talent, scenes shot, and adherence to union rules.

Set Production Assistant
GDC Television in conjunction with
Let Her Rip Productions, Orlando, FL   2001

- Followed the orders of the first and second assistant directors.
- In charge of 2 other production assistants for maintaining crowd control on exterior shots.

[Where were you educated or trained?]

EDUCATION
A.A. in Mass Communications, John Blue Community College, Miami, FL

These two résumés show the formula for organizing your Fearless Résumé. You don't have to include the optional blocks unless they apply to you. You do have a great deal of latitude and choice in formatting your résumé, but do stick to this basic template and you're sure to succeed.

The Conversational Approach to Résumé Writing

If you ever feel "stuck" on your résumé and want to get back on track, take a look at the question being asked for the section you're working on. You may even imagine a real person asking the question. Your mind will automatically respond.

This lively question-and-answer approach keeps your imagination fresh as to what the employer wants. *A fearless résumé is therefore about "you and me" rather than just "me, me, me."*

- Rather than being a monologue, as most résumés are, a Fearless Résumé is in fact a *conversation* in which we predict and then answer the questions that the employer naturally has on her mind.

This gets the reader involved and makes your résumé vital and refreshing. It's the responsive and precise way that you will learn to answer these queries that will turn your Fearless Résumé into the roadway to your interview!

Sound good? Okay. I'd bet you'd like to see a Fearless Résumé in action. Let's have a look at a sample résumé and see how the answers to the basic five questions fit on the page.

The questions on the résumés, which appeared earlier in this chapter, are there for you to see and learn from, but you don't actually write the questions on the résumé itself. The sections written in italics are also just guidelines. The italicized sentences should not be written on your real résumé.

Next, I am going to show you some of the optional blocks mentioned earlier. If you have a need for these blocks, use them. If not, they can be left out.

- You'll see plenty of résumés with just the basic blocks *and* some with optional blocks in Chapter 10.

Optional Blocks

For review, optional blocks that *can* be included on your résumé but are not mandatory are

1. Relevant skills (sometimes called "technical skills" or "professional skills")
2. Professional affiliations
3. Publications and patents
4. Awards

Would you like to see some more Fearless Résumés, or are you ready to put pen to paper already?

Either way, you're on your way to producing a fantastic piece of writing. Further examples of Fearless Résumés are provided for you in the last chapter, if you'd like to take a peek at them before you write your own.

CHAPTER 8

Tips for a Terrific Résumé

"*Confidence . . . is directness and courage in meeting the facts of life.*"

—John Dewey

Okay, you've hit the mark. There are only a few more details to remember. Again, congratulations for caring enough about yourself, your time, and your chosen occupation to learn the state-of-the-art Fearless Résumé.

Yours is a document that will give you an unbeatable start in your job search and a true edge on your competition; it is a marketable, sellable, provable depiction of yourself and your skills that will never, ever bore the reader.

In fact, in the first ten seconds, your document will stop your reader in her tracks and instill within her the *emotional* desire to hire you. In the rest of your petition, she will discover the logical clarity behind this and the survival instinct that leads her to want to have you on her team.

Now it's time for you to compose your own Fearless Résumé, using a template (partly blank form) that I've used with over 15,000 people, from entry-level to executive and from age 18 to 75.

Before you set pen to paper or sit down at your computer, however, let me review some quick tips that will ensure your credibility and make your Fearless Résumé flow seamlessly.

Tips for Your Contact Block

Don't use a nickname. *Do* use your full name. A middle initial or middle name is optional.

For example, write "Bud Smith" rather than "Bud 'the Stud' Smith" or "Bud 'Buddy' Smith."

Of course, this example is quite farfetched, but you wouldn't believe how many silly nicknames I've seen or heard about on résumés!

Basically, using this kind of nickname is a turnoff and will serve only to diminish the importance of your document. Once you get the job, if you would like your coworkers or your boss to refer to you by your nickname, that's fine. Just don't make him try to swallow the nickname before he gets to know you in person or before you get the job.

The same goes for e-mail addresses.

Some of the far-out ones I've seen are rocketman4563@thataway.com and ladyloveyou9835@netscore.net.

E-mail addresses with catchy or clever elements like that are fun to use with your friends and family, but they really are not dignified enough for a résumé.

Try not to use the e-mail address of the company that you currently work for.

If you use the e-mail address of the company you are still working for, watch out. An e-mail address like guy.henry@companyIstillworkfor.net will raise understandable suspicions that you are using your own desk, your own time, and your company's time and resources to conduct your own personal business. This is something that is strictly frowned upon. Even if your former company allows you to use their resouces, it is wise to refrain from using your old e-mail address because you never know how the prospective employer will react.

- If the prospective employer sees that you've taken up the habit of wasting your present employer's time, why should he expect that you wouldn't do the same if you were hired to work for his company?

Do use an *11 or 12 point Times New Roman or Arial regular (not bold or italic) font.* Don't use any fancy graphics, typefaces, large-sized letters, or layout. This kind of style, however artistic it may look, is really more confusing to the potential employer and makes the résumé harder to read.

Take the time to get an e-mail address that is *both* personalized to you and professional.

If you're going for a more professional impression, try getting an e-mail account with Yahoo!, hotmail, gmail, Comcast, AOL, or some other free e-mail provider, and pick something that resembles your own name, such as janicegold@freee-mail-provider.com.

Do use a regular street address. Don't use a P.O. box, if at all possible. Although the use of a post office box may serve to protect your privacy, employers often view it with suspicion.

Do use a professional-sounding answering machine or voice mail system with a clear and dignified message. Finally, just a tip: for whatever phone number(s)— home, office, mobile, or toll free—you are listing in the name block on your résumé, be sure that they are equipped with a *professional-sounding message* (without dogs barking, kids yelling, traffic sounds, music, or other distractions).

The simplest message to leave would be something in your own voice (not a mechanical or prerecorded voice if possible) that says:

> "Hello. You've reached Bob Winston at 243-777-7877. Thank you for calling. Please leave a complete message after the tone, including your phone number and the best time to reach you."

Again, *after* you get the job, you can put a more personal or fun touch on your message, but for now, keep it simple and to the point. Try to get an answering machine or voice mail system that allows you to check messages remotely if you are not near your phone so that you'll stay on top of your messages and be able to return calls promptly. Employers absolutely love to get a quick response. It shows that you're efficient and enthusiastic about the job.

You might also consider a call forwarding system, so that if the employer calls your home phone, for example, the call will be automatically forwarded to your cell phone so that you can answer it immediately.

Call forwarding is also available on most cell phones. Call your local phone company or cell phone provider to arrange for one of these easy and inexpensive systems while you're job hunting.

Tips for Your Objective Block

When you're submitting a résumé as a direct response to a printed or Internet ad, *always* use the job title that is used in the job posting. For the reader, who, you remember, may have 350 résumés on his desk or in his inbox, it is annoying to say the least to have to wonder what job you're applying for. As much as you may like to think that the person will read your résumé and find the best "fit" for you in his company, that is *not* his job, and it is extremely rare for a busy recruiter or hiring manager to afford you that favor. Even when you post your résumé on a job board or Web site, hoping that many readers for many companies will view it, you must *still* include some sort of job title. So, in the case of a résumé submission to *one* company for a particular job, if your Fearless Résumé has the title Financial Advisor and the job offered is for a Financial Consultant, you *must* take the little bit of extra time to go back into your résumé and change the job title for this company. It is both a courtesy to the company and an indication that you're serious about applying for *that* particular job in that particular company. Hiring managers like to know that you've put thought into singling out their company because you specifically want to work there. Having no objective or using the wrong words in your objective when you're applying directly for an advertised position indicates that you were careless and did not really *choose* that company at all.

Word Choice

A résumé is a *living* document.

You don't get to write it once and then use the same thing forever. You may change it many times in one job search and several times during your working life.

It is wise to have the words—*all* the words—conform to the verbiage in the job description as much as possible.

So, if the job description mentions Information Technology several times, and the first draft of your résumé refers to the same thing as Computer Science, then by all means change your résumé.

- Some researchers have shown that the more closely the expressions in your résumé mirror the wording in the job description, the better your chances of getting interviewed.

This rule does not apply when you're talking about official degrees and certificates. Do not change the name of an official degree.

Dates

If you've been using months *and* years when presenting your work history, try this little trick (which is completely acceptable on modern résumés, by the way). Do *not* use the months on your résumé at all. Let's look at a sample of a hypothetical job for which you note *both* the months and the years that you worked there and compare it to including *only* the years that you were at the position.

Example of months and years:

| Job Title, Company, | December 2006– |
| City, State | January 2007 |

How long does it look like you were at that company? You're right—about one month. A very short stay at a particular company raises suspicion in the eyes of the employer. Were you "job hopping"—just looking around casually and leaving if the job didn't work out for you?

- Did you quit prematurely? Were you fired? Could you not adjust to your responsibilities or to the personalities of those you were working with? Did you quarrel with your boss or your supervisor?

What happened, and why did you stay for only a month? Are you afraid of commitment? Are you unable to keep your word? All of these fears and more enter the employer's mind when he sees one, two, or a pattern of short stays at positions.

Although, in my own opinion, you have a right to leave a job for almost any reason whenever you wish, most employers don't see it that way, and it makes sense from their perspective. As you already read, when you put together all the time it takes to do the advertising, paperwork, interviewing, and training of a new hire, it can cost the employer well over $10,000 and sometimes much more.

When a company is making an investment like that, it wants you to stay *at least* long enough for it to get a return on its investment—that is, profitable productivity from your efforts.

I don't have any judgment if you have a "choppy" work history. There are a host of reasons, including family issues, marital separation or discord, medical problems, disability, emotional upset, financial challenges, addiction, harassment on the job, trouble with the law, layoffs, company closures or reorganization, travel or study opportunities, or just simply changing your mind, that may make the work history on your résumé not look as smooth as you would like it to be. The point is, most people, whether you know it or not, have some gaps in their employment history.

The very idea that people should have a perfectly smooth and untainted record of service from the time they graduate from high school or college until the time they retire is unfair and absurd. It's not often that real life works that way.

Still, most companies frown upon obvious gaps in your employment history, and they may pass your résumé by or ask about these gaps at the interview if you don't do something about them on your résumé. Fortunately, there are ways to tackle this problem and still maintain your integrity without having to lie. Three of them are

1. Listing only years on your résumé
2. Omitting certain jobs, if possible
3. Indicating on the résumé what you were doing and/or that you are willing to discuss a gap of more than one year at the interview

Listing Only Years on Your Résumé

Let's look at each of these solutions one by one. Remember the example of the person's résumé that indicated that she had worked for only one month at a company? Here it is again:

Job Title, Company,   December 2006–
City, State   January 2007

Now, what if we omit the months and use only the years of employment?

Job Title, Company,   2006–2007
City, State

Much better, isn't it? It's even possible that the person was at that job from January 2006 to December 2007—almost *two* years.

- On a job application, you must write the year, the month, and sometimes even the day that your employment began and ended. Fortunately, this is not necessary on a résumé unless the employer specifically requests it, which is very rare.

Omitting a Job from Your Résumé

Let's look at an example of omitting a job from your employment history.

October 2005–December 2008

June 2005–August 2005

June 2001–May 2005

Take a look at what happens when we omit the middle job, then delete the months and use only years:

2005-2008

2001–2005

Unless the short job in the summer of 2005 (in the middle) is *absolutely essential* to the job you're seeking, I recommend that you leave it out. We've already listed some of the many reasons that jobs can end. If your shorter job ended for any of those reasons, it's within your rights and definitely to your advantage to put it behind you.

Explain at Interview

If you have a gap of two years or more between positions, it's better to say on your résumé that you're willing to explain the gap than it is to ignore it. This is very simply done.

2008–present

Will explain at interview.   2004–2008

2000–2004

Dates for More than One Job at a Company

There is another way to make your dates look smooth and make your tenure at a company where you've had *more* than one job title seem longer.

Mary Lou Smith
222 XXX Drive
Honolulu, HI XXXXX
(808) 344-XXXX

Objective: XXXXX

Summary: XXXXX

Employment History
JJL Inc., Honolulu, HI   **1999–2008**

      Human Resources Director (2003–2008)
      Human Resources Manager (2001–2003)
      Human Resources Representative (1999–2001)

Education: XXXX

- When you've had more than one position, list your cumulative (largest) span of years in bold type and the time you spent at each particular job title in parentheses in a regular typeface.

Dates on Your Education

Your reader may be prejudiced on the grounds that you are either too young or too old if you list the dates of your education, so please leave those dates blank. Do list education in progress.

Blocks You Should Not Use

Hobbies

Notice that we do *not* include a hobbies block. Listing hobbies is an old-fashioned custom that is outmoded today. You may think that using it makes you look like a well-rounded person (which, to some degree, it does), but in a modern résumé, including hobbies and other personal information is unnecessary and detracts from the image of the professional "you" that your résumé is going to portray. It's best not to mention your hobbies, even if you think they make you unique.

Mentioning your hobbies can sometimes backfire on you if the employer disapproves of certain activities or believes that the time you spend pursuing your outside interests might detract from your time or focus on the job.

Don't let the temptation to test the open-mindedness of the reader ruin your chances to make a living. Perhaps when you've been hired and your employer and colleagues know you better, you can have fun sharing more of your personal side by talking about or even inviting others to participate in some of your hobbies.

References

You also do not need to write your references' names and phone numbers on your document. Likewise, including a phrase like "References Available upon Request," which is a very common mistake, is actually redundant and does not belong on your Fearless Résumé. The employer knows that he can request your references if necessary.

When You've Finished Writing

Be sure to use spell check *and* have someone else *read* (not judge) your résumé to correct any errors that may be lurking there. As I said, it's almost impossible for *everyone* to agree that any résumé is perfect, but let's make sure we get your Fearless Résumé as close to the highest goal as possible. After all, your Fearless Résumé is about you, and it's time to show the world *just how incredible you are*.

Now, let's move ahead where you'll find a template for writing your *own* Fearless Résumé to make sure it's the best it can be.

Your Name
Your Street Address
City, State, Zip Code
Home phone:
Cell phone:
E-mail address:

Objective: A position as a(n) _____.

Summary: (power proposition)

Over _____ years (or *knowledge of, proficient in,* or *competent in*)
as a(n) _____ in the _____ industry, specializing
in _____, _____, and _____.

Write a Q statement here. _____.

[Optional] Write another Q statement here. _____
_____.

[Optional] Write one or two degrees and/or one or two certifications or licenses here (write current progress in education if
applicable). _____
_____.

And/or [optional] write one or two awards here. _____
_____.

And/or [optional] write one or two professional affiliations here.
_____.

And/or write three applicable personal characteristics here:
_____, _____, and _____.

[Optional] Relevant Skills. To make a skills box using Microsoft
Office, go to the top of the screen to "Table." Click on it and find
a drop-down menu. Click on "Draw Table" and find a pop-up
toolbar. Go to the small picture of a table that says "Insert Table"
when you place your cursor over it. Click on the icon and see a
pop-up box called "Insert Table." Choose the number of columns
(horizontal) and rows (vertical) that you would like to have in
your table, then press "OK." List 6 to 12 skills.

SKILL	SKILL	SKILL
SKILL	SKILL	SKILL

Employment History (put last job first)
Job Title
Company Name, City, State   **2003–Present**

- Write two to six Q statements with a simple round bullet (under "Format" in MS Word). Even if you already used a Q statement in your power proposition, write it here under the job in which it was accomplished.

- XXX _____

_____

_____.

- XXX _____

_____

_____.

- XXX _____

_____

_____.

- XXX _____

_____

_____.

- XXX _____

_____

_____.

- XXX _____

_____

_____.

(Continue to do this for previous positions going back no more than 10 to 15 years. For very old jobs, you may need only two bullets. If a job is more than 10 years ago, you may put zero bullets if you wish.)

Job Title
Company Name, City, State   2003

- XXX _____

  _____

  _____.

- XXX _____

  _____

  _____.

- XXX _____

  _____

  _____.

- XXX _____

  _____

  _____.

Your first initial, last name, p. 2

Job Title
Company Name, City, State   1997–2002

- XXX _____

  _____

  _____.

- XXX _____

  _____

  _____.

Job Title
Company Name, City, State   1995–1997

Education. Even though you may have stated this in your power proposition, you need to write it here too.

Put highest education first

Publications and Patents

Awards

       _____ Achievement Award

       Awarded for _____

       Recognized for _____

       Received bonus for _____

       Best _____ Award

Professional Affiliations

       Member in good standing of _____

       Member of _____

       Honorary member of _____

       Charter member of _____

       Student member of _____

       Affiliate member of _____

       Professional member of _____

       Union member, Local #_____

Note: There is no need to write "Hobbies" or "References Available upon Request."

CHAPTER 9

Your Moment
of Triumph

> *"Courage is the most important of all virtues, because without it we can't practice any other virtue with consistency."*
>
> —Maya Angelou

This is your big moment. You know your skills; you can quantify your accomplishments; and, most of all, you know how to emotionally capture and keep your readers' attention. I'm truly proud of you! Now, it's *your* turn to write your own Fearless Résumé.

So that you won't have to flip through the book to find all the great work you've done, the page numbers of the essential sections are provided here so that you can refer to them as you construct your document.

My power proposition   p. 16

My general skills   p. 63

My job-specific skills   p. 68

My personal characteristics   p. 72

My Q statements   p. 80

Your résumé may change several times over the course of your job search and many times throughout your life. But now you have a formula, a strategy, and insight into what employers are looking for that most of your competitors don't. Now, here's a blank template for you to use to construct your first Fearless Résumé! Begin by filling in the contact block.

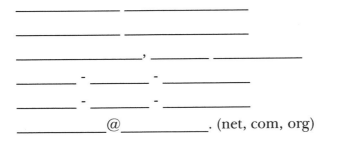

OBJECTIVE

_____

_____

_____

SUMMARY

_____

_____

_____

_____

_____

_____

WORK HISTORY

_____

_____

_____

_____

_____

_____

_____

_____

_____

_____

_____

_____

_____

_____

_____

_____

_____

_____

_____

_____

EDUCATION

_____

_____

_____

_____

_____

[Optional Blocks: please insert in the template in the proper place.]

RELEVANT SKILLS

PUBLICATIONS/PATENTS

_____

_____

_____

_____

_____

AWARDS AND RECOGNITIONS

_____

_____

PROFESSIONAL GROUPS AND AFFILIATIONS

_____

_____

OTHER

You've done a terrific job! But let's not stop here. As one of my very special *Fearless Résumés* readers, you can visit my Web site or e-mail me at to get free information on other areas of your job search, such as how to bypass human resources and get directly to the hiring manager, how to ascend to the highest rungs of your ability in an interview, and how to negotiate up to 20 percent more than the initial offer, as well as a host of job search and career transition information.

I want to see you through this whole process, until the time when you get the offer you're looking for and can run somewhere private and scream, "I did it!" Well, I might not see you. But I will be waiting to hear your scream of triumph reach me all the way to California.

All the best to you in your life and in your job search.

CHAPTER 10

Sample Résumés

> *"I long to accomplish a great and noble task, but it is my chief duty to accomplish small tasks as if they were great and noble."*
>
> —Helen Keller

Adrian Takahana, Esq.   Home Phone: (208) 293-XXXX
XXX East Stokey Road   Cell Phone: (210) 367-XXXX
Carlsbad, TX 855XX   atjd2000@elevation.com

Objective
Corporate counsel position in the Fortune 500 sector.

Professional Expertise
Over 10 years as corporate counsel to Fortune 500 companies, including 4TEL Technologies and IBX Systems, specializing in complex business and corporate contracts, risk
reduction, licenses, and transactions. Negotiated and provided legal documentation for over 150 customer agreements in transactions of up to $150 million. Awarded 4TEL
Performance Achievement honors in 2005 and 2006. Juris
Doctor (J.D.), Oxmore University; B.A. in Economics with
Highest Honors. Trilingual in English, Japanese, and Can-
tonese. *Willing to pay for own relocation costs anywhere in United
States or Asia.*

Employment Experience

<u>Director, Legal Department</u>
4TEL Inc., Austin, TX   2000–2009

- Provided risk management oversight for 4TEL Capital
  Sales, Operations, and Credit groups.
- Negotiated major customer agreements of up to $150
  million per transaction.
- Represented 4TEL in cross-functional business development, maintaining existing accounts and winning over
  86 new accounts in a 7-year period.
- Restructured existing legal process by developing,
  training, and delegating to dedicated in-house legal
  group, saving the company approximately 3 attorney
  salaries at an average sum of $235,000 each per
  year.

- Provided training to subordinates on risk reduction and taught business success tools to decrease litigation by 25%, thereby saving an average of $160 million per year.
- Created streamlined templates for contracts paperwork that saved an average of 6 hours per week per attorney.

Attorney
IBX Computers, Richmond, VA   1994–2000

- Oversaw entire southwestern United States, conducting transactions of up to $100 million.
- Represented Financial, Commercial, Health Care, and Government lines of business.
- Structured government transaction to avoid litigation from a competitor that saved up to $13 million.
- Avoided numerous class action suits and served as prelitigation counsel and mediator.

Prior Legal Experience
Adrian Takahana, Esq.
Private practice in Washington, D.C., specializing in contract law.

Education
Admitted: U.S. Supreme Court

Admitted: State of Maryland

Juris Doctor degree: Oxmore University,
Baltimore, Maryland

Bachelor of Arts degree in Economics:
Southern Maryland University

Sarah L. Porter   (804) 237- XXXX Home
2XX Helmsly Lane   (804) 772- XXXX Mobile
Cincinnati, Ohio 4XXXX   porter_sl373@relay.net

Objective

A position as a physical therapist aide (intern).

Summary

Competence as a Certified Physical Therapist Aide gained from a 1-year accredited college-level program. Graduated with a 3.8 grade point average including academic and practical applications of being a physical therapist aide. Empathetic, motivated, good rapport with patients.

Relevant Classes

- Human Anatomy
- Human Physiology
- Physical Therapy Practices
- Ethics and Laws Governing Physical Therapists
- Kinesiology
- Medical Terminology
- Musculoskeletal Systems
- Common Injuries and Conditions
- Introduction to Exercise Physiology
- Patient Psychology
- Administrative Procedures

Work History

<u>Server</u>

Hamlet's Restaurant, Akron, Ohio   2007–2009

- Performed a part-time job to save and pay for school.
- Handled as many as 25 customers per shift.
- Carried out cash and credit card transactions.

Education

Certificate as a Physical Therapist Aide, Hollick College, Akron, Ohio

Professional Affiliations

Association for Physical Therapy Professionals (student membership)

James F. Harris
17XX Helen Street
Willets, WY 351XX
(300) 737-XXXX
jfh@wintercom.net

Objective:
A position in customer service.

Summary

Over 3 years progressively responsible experience in customer service in the restaurant and retail industries. Specialties include retail sales, store displays, and cash register operation. Undergraduate studies at Eli Fuller College, Menton, WY. Currently enrolled in a course of study leading to completion of the Dale Carnegie Sales seminar series. Fast learner, people person, polite and organized.

Relevant Skills

Retail sales	Phone sales	Department displays
Inventory control	Customer Service	Cash register
Employee training	Credit card transactions	Employee supervision

Employment History

Salesperson, Tracy's Department Store, Willets, WY
2008–present

- In charge of the men's sportswear department, which includes approximately 1,000 pieces of inventory.

- Achieved highest sales of February 2009 for all clothing departments.

- Handle up to 350 customers weekly.

- Operate the cash register and accept credit cards for up to $700 per purchase.

- Arrange clothing on the racks and displays in order to attract customers.

- Calculate returns and chargebacks.

<u>Waiter</u>, Hanley's Country Kitchen, Benfanto, WY
2006–2008

- Took orders and served from a menu of over 60 items.

- Served individuals, couples, families, and larger banquets of up to 40 people.

- Operated the cash register and processed credit cards.

- Received the "punctuality" award for never being late to work in all of 2007.

Education and Certifications

Courses, Eli Fuller College, Menton, WY

Currently enrolled in Dale Carnegie Sales seminar series, Lowe, WY

Cindy Nelson SPHR
273X 3rd Street. Boston, MA 022XX
617-206-XXXX cell 617-459-XXXX home
cindynhr@doubletech.net

OBJECTIVE
Senior Human Resources Manager/Organizational Development.

PROFESSIONAL SUMMARY
Over 8 years as a human resource professional specializing in consulting, organizational behavior, and recruiting. Performed intervention strategies with Technical Assistance Center at Boston Scientific to diagnose underlying issues and facilitate problem resolution for team and management dynamics, directly improving self-reported employee satisfaction from 3 to 4.2 on a scale of 1 to 5. Increased employee retention by 25% at Goldman Capital, saving the company many thousands of dollars on new hiring procedures. B.A. in Business Administration, Channel University; currently pursuing coursework leading to a Master of Science in Organization Development at Boston University. Thesis topic: "Employee Behavior during Mergers and Acquisitions." SPHR. Member, Society for Human Resources Management, Boston Human Resource Association, American Society for Training and Development.

EMPLOYMENT HISTORY
Sr. Human Resources Manager
Boston Scientific Corporation, Fremont, CA   2005–present

- Led new manager assimilation process through team facilitation, resulting in shorter ramp-up period, saving the company as much as $10,000 per first month salary for manager level and above.

- Provided employee relations support to management and employees, performing investigations and recommendations that effectively saved the company over $100 million by deescalating potential lawsuits.

- Recruited to provide generalist support for client groups ranging from 175 to 300 technical, scientific, and support associates.

- Drove high-volume planning and recruiting methodologies with staffing teams by ensuring that superior candidates were being sourced and selected within preferred deadlines.

- Worked with Human Factors to ensure compliance with the Americans with Disabilities Act.

<u>Human Resources Manager</u>
Goldman Capital, Boston, MA   2004

- Increased employee retention by 25%, saving the company money on new hiring procedures.
- Mentored 33 new hire sales associates and assisted with the development of business plans.
- Utilized Recruitmax to source and recruit for 175 branches of this $2 billion East Coast mortgage brokerage firm, recognized as #803 in the Fortune 1000.
- Managed administrative staff of 3: 1 administrative assistant, 1 HR intern, and 1 HR specialist.

<u>Human Resource Generalist</u>
Valenti Manufacturing, Townsend, MA   2001–2004

- Led and supported human resources team of 5 members in the functional areas of employee relations, recruiting, training and development, compensation and benefits, HRIS, and general human resources.
- Managed over 12 community giving events per year in conjunction with marketing teams.

EDUCATION AND TRAINING
Currently completing a course of study leading to an MS in Organizational Behavior. Thesis topic: "Employee Behavior during Mergers and Acquisitions."
Boston University

BS, Business Administration
Channel University, Rochester, NY

PROFESSIONAL AFFILIATIONS
SPHR Certification
Society for Human Resource Management
American Society for Training and Development

Harvey S. Sumner
XXX August Drive
Memphis, TN 34XXX
Home Phone: (777) 333-3333
Cell Phone: (777) 444-4443
harveys@doitnow.net

Objective

A position as a sales manager in the
automotive rental industry.

Professional Summary

Over 6 years experience as a manager in the automotive and trucking industries, specializing in team leadership, operations, and employee training. Exceeded monthly quotas by an average of 22% over a 4-year period while serving as manager at ABC Car and Truck Rentals. Attained a 4.9-star customer satisfaction rating based on a survey of approximately 600 customer responses per year. A.S. in Industrial Technology, Tennessee State College, Memphis, TN. Reliable, personable, goal-oriented.

Employment History

Branch Manager
ABC Automotive, Turnpike, TN   2004–present

- Manage a branch of airport car and truck rental business with over 305 vehicles.
- Train and supervise 4 rental personnel and 2 customer service representatives.
- Maintain top-quality inventory by directing a cleaning and maintenance staff of 9.
- Sell and upsell car rental packages to exceed monthly quotas by an average of 22%.

- Record and track inventory and accounts receivable with specialized software.
- Interface with up to 25 customers per day, with a customer satisfaction rating of 4.9 stars

<u>Weight Master Assistant Manager</u>
Washington Manufacturing, Wahlog, TN   2003–2004

- Performed data entry tracking on loads of up to 2 tons of materials and cargo.
- Applied mathematical calculations to balance incoming and outgoing truck weight.
- Operated and maintained designated equipment with a Class A License.
- Utilized Hazardous Materials certification to ensure safe and nontoxic cargo, keeping loads under 100% government compliance at periodic spot checks.

Education and Training

A.S., Industrial Technology, Tennessee State College, Memphis, TN

Class A license from XYZ Transportation Institute, Memphis, TN

Hazardous Materials Certificate from University of Tennessee Extension Program

Melanie Isaac, MS
120 South Milton Avenue   Phone: (804) 576-XXXX
Healdsburg, AZ 75XXX   m.isaac@healdsburbgcounty.gov

OBJECTIVE

A teaching position in environmental health or public health administration.

SUMMARY OF QUALIFICATIONS

Over 15 years experience in environmental health and safety, specializing in site safety, community preparedness, and overseeing health and safety for large private and public projects. Received a Mayor's Community Excellence Service award for effective program design policies, procedures, and protocols on over 8 project sites. Saved over 7 facilities while ensuring the use of appropriate procedures for the safest and most cost-effective results. Lecturer in Environmental Studies, Camelback College.

PROFESSIONAL EXPERIENCE

Senior Environmental Health and Safety Specialist
Health and Human Services Department,
County of Healdsburg, AZ   1990–Present

- Developed and implemented nationally recognized health and safety programs.
- Created and implemented an employee Emergency Response Training program, achieving 100% compliance with county and state regulations.
- Led team in development and implementation of comprehensive employee drug and alcohol testing program with 100% compliance with target.
- Advised teams of construction management personnel, individual site coordinators, and client EH&S personnel, including those from hospital projects, to develop specific plans appropriate to each site, protecting workers from exposure to hazardous/infectious materials.
- Team leader for individual site safety coordinators to monitor and enforce safety compliance.

- Administrator for regional air quality and water control compliance, resulting in zero citations.

PREVIOUS POSITIONS

Lecturer in Environmental Studies, Camelback College, Tempe, AZ
Keynote Speaker, Urban Ecology Conference, Chicago, IL

EDUCATION AND CERTIFICATIONS

- M.S., Environmental Studies, with Honors, Saint Peter's University, Phoenix, AZ
- B.A., Public Health, Pennsylvania Polytechnic State University, Philadelphia, PA
- Fed-OSHA Construction Safety Instructor
- Fed-OSHA Hazardous Waste Operations and Emergency Response

PUBLICATIONS (COMPLETE LIST OF PUBLICATIONS AVAILABLE UPON REQUEST)

"Environmental Issues in Securing Ideal Level Water Tables," *Journal of Integrated Ecology*, June 2003.

"Optimizing Budgets for Hazardous Waste Removal," *Environmental Quarterly*, Fall 2000.

"Student-Centered Methods for Teaching Cost-Effective and Compliant Subdivision Construction," *American Journal of City Planning*, January 1998.

"Impact Studies for City and County Recreation Facilities," *Journal of Parklands and Recreation*, September 1997.

Thomas Hernandez
222 South Drive
Jonesmore, Iowa

Home phone: (608) 342-XXXX
Mobile phone: (608) 477-XXXX
E-mail: hernandez_t@njtek.com

Professional Expertise

Over 10 years director-level leadership experience in the Information Technology field, specializing in global network design and engineering, leading broad-based functional teams, and managing multimillion-dollar budgets. Reengineered global information technology infrastructure in less than 47 days after dangerous fragmentation, thus exceeding the previous internal customer satisfaction by 22%, to a rating of 89%. Centralized and implemented database functionality to 19 regional sites and Asian subsidiaries. Electrical MSEE, MBA with an emphasis in technology leadership with honors. Member of the American Information Technology Society.

Relevant Technical Skills

Operating Systems/Systems Management/Security
CP/M, PC/MS-DOS, Apple System 7.x, Windows (3.x, WFW, 95, 98, NT 3.x, Vista)
Symantec Antivirus, Compaq Insight Manager, Business Continuity, Risk Tolerance
Content filters, firewalls

Hardware
Compaq servers, Dell servers, Apple II-Macintosh External Storage
SCSI, USB, IBM SNA controllers, Cisco routers, printers
Fault-tolerance, redundancy, RAID storage
Remote access, wireless, telecom
TCP/IP Suite, 3COM, Wang Net, EtherTalk, Netware 2-3.x, MS-NT Server, 10BT, 10B2, Phone Net, Ethernet, NetBIOS

Software/Languages
MS SQL, dBase, FoxPro, MS Access, Lotus 123, MS Office Pro, Lotus Notes
MS Exchange, Notes Mail, Eudora, MS Project, MS Outlook
Netscape, MS Internet Server
MS SQL, BASIC, MS VB, HTML

Platforms
Linux
UNIX

Professional Experience

Director Information Systems
Blue Sky Integrated Systems, Des Moines, IA   2001–2009

- Planning and implementing LAN/WAN network design and engineering.
- IT capital budget of $3.5 million over 3 years.
- Reengineered global information technology infrastructure in less than 47 days after dangerous fragmentation.
- Established facilities in China and Latin America and necessary IT infrastructure, including applications servers, connectivity, e-mail, etc.
- Centralized and implemented database functionality to 19 regional sites and Asian subsidiaries.
- Internal customers satisfied, evidenced by management reports of 89% success ratings and independent audits.

Manager, Information Technology
Efficace, San Dimas, CA   1994–2000

- Managed networking operations in five divisions.
- Led a team of 550 employees/clients in Phoenix, San Francisco, Atlanta, and Lisbon.
- Planned and implemented budget of $2.1 million per year.
- Initiated end-user feedback system that saved an average of $81,000 per year.
- Eliminated downtime in the manufacturing and operations divisions by 18%, thereby saving up to $46,000 per month in costs.

Degrees & Certifications

Microsoft Certified Professional, Harris Data Systems

M.B.A. (technology emphasis), University of Phoenix Online

M.S.E.E., University of California at Long Beach

B.A., Economics, Eastern Michigan University

Professional Affiliations

Member of the American Information Technology

President, Technology Education Fund for Disadvantaged Youth

Joshua Kennedy
43XX Autumn Court, Apt. C
Tilden, NH 23XXX

307-722-XXXX mobile
321-826-XXXX direct
kennedy_josh4002@oog.com

Objective: A position as a network administrator.

Summary: Over 6 years experience in electrical engineering, specializing in LAN/WAN networking, testing and hardware/software validation, installation, and removal. Created over 9 test plans and spreadsheets for different products to capture complete test cases required for specifications and customer requirements. Reduced system downtime by 18% and increased sensitivity of the inspection systems, saving tens of thousands of dollars. A.A. in Electronics; currently enrolled in classes to obtain a Network Administrator Certificate, N.S.F.E.E.

Technical Skills

LAN/WAN networking	Flash BIOS upgrades	PCB layout and design
Failure analysis	Stress tests	Defect tracking
Install/remove HW/SW	Troubleshooting	SW/HW validation

Employment History

QA Test Engineer
Banana Belt Technologies, Binghamton, NH   2007–present

- Debugging process and failure analysis down to component level.
- Set up test equipment and product under the test in the manufacturing for control run performance test.
- Created over 9 test plans and spreadsheets for different products to capture complete test cases required for specifications and customer requirements.
- Regression, integration, and system-level test execution.

- Performed complex hardware calibrations on new products, finding failures before releasing product to the customers.
- Helped IT engineers with building new PCs or upgrading for R&D engineers, including BIOS upgrades, installing licensed operating/debugging software, various hardware required for diagnostics or functional testing process, and configuring dial-up, LAN/WAN networks.

Manufacturing Assistant Engineer
Center Stage Electronics, Las Vegas, NV   2003–2007

- Conducted failure analysis and repair of printed circuit boards (alignment, memory, autofocus, laser's preamp, motor driver PCBs, and more) down to component level on multimillion-dollar equipment.
- Performed optical and laser alignments, electronic calibrations, and electromechanical adjustments to meet sensitivity qualifications.
- Reduced system downtime by 18% and increased sensitivity of the inspection systems.
- Initiated several test procedures in regard to systems assembly and subassembly troubleshooting, mechanical and electromechanical calibrations, and laser alignment.

Education

Currently enrolled in classes to obtain a Network Administrator Certificate, N.S.F.E.E, Hartmond, NH

A.S., Northeast Technical Institute, Bellevue, NH

INDEX

ABOUT THE AUTHOR

Marky Stein has been a career coach and public speaker for over two decades, working with entry level to professional job seekers from more than 75 Fortune 500 companies. She currently runs a private career coaching practice in Northern California. Author of the career classic *Fearless Interviewing*, Stein is also the online interview expert at Monster.com. Visit her at www.markystein.com.

Marky Stein is a career coach and the author of:

Fearless Interviewing:
How to Win the Job by Communicating With Confidence
(McGraw-Hill 2003)

Fearless Career Change:
The Fast Track to Success in a New Field
(McGraw-Hill 2005)

Get a Great Job When You Don't Have a Job:
From Hopeless to Fearless
(McGraw-Hill October 2009)

She also owns and operates a
private career coaching practice in California.
Visit her at www.markystein.com